Narrative of the Life of Henry Box Brown

NARRATIVE

OF THE

LIFE OF HENRY BOX BROWN

WRITTEN BY HIMSELF

Introduction by Richard Newman

Foreword by Henry Louis Gates, Jr.

OXFORD
UNIVERSITY PRESS
2002

OXFORD

UNIVERSITY PRESS

Oxford New York
Auckland   Bangkok   Buenos Aires
Cape Town   Chennai   Dar es Salaam   Delhi   Hong Kong
Istanbul   Karachi   Kolkata   Kuala Lumpur   Madrid
Melbourne   Mexico City   Mumbai   Nairobi   Sao Paulo
Shanghai   Singapore   Taipei   Tokyo   Toronto

and an associated company in Berlin

Foreword copyright © 2002 by Henry Louis Gates, Jr.
Copyright © 2002 by Oxford University Press, Inc.

First published by Oxford University Press, Inc.
198 Madison Avenue, New York, New York 10016

Library of Congress Cataloging-in-Publication Data
Brown, Henry Box, b. 1816
The narrative of the life of Henry Box Brown /
written by himself ; introduction by Richard Newman ;
foreword by Henry Louis Gates, Jr.
p.   cm.   Includes bibliographical references and index.
ISBN 978-0-19-514854-1
1. Brown, Henry Box, b. 1816.
2. Fugitive slaves—Virginia—Biography.
3. African Americans—Virginia—Biography.
4. Slavery—Virginia—History.
5. African American abolitionists—Biography.
I. Title.
E450 .B873 2002   305.5'67'092—dc21   [B]   2001055421

Printed in the United States of America
on acid-free paper

Contents

Foreword

by Henry Louis Gates, Jr.

*O*ne of the most curious, and fascinating, genres of literature is that created in America by fugitive black slaves. The very idea that slaves could, or would, escape from bondage, flee mostly on foot to the North, live in peril of slave-catchers in search of the heavy bounties offered for their return, and then, audaciously, write autobiographical narratives of their time in bondage, their escape, and their new lives as free women and men proved endlessly fascinating to the American and British reading public. These slave narratives, as a genre, as many scholars have demonstrated, were hugely popular, especially between 1850—the date of the passage of the Fugitive Slave Act—and the end of the Civil War.

Several were best-sellers; most were extremely well reviewed and widely discussed, both for their considerable political value in the abolitionists' struggle against slavery, and for their significance as a novel genre of literature. Names such as William Wells Brown, Frederick Douglass, Josiah Henson, Linda Brent, and William and Ellen Craft—among dozens of others—were regularly included among the literary lions of the decade preceding the Civil War. And of these ex-slave authors, none rendered a story more curiously compelling—and incredible—than did Henry "Box" Brown.

As difficult as it may be for us to believe, Henry Box Brown mailed himself from slavery to freedom. Whereas other slaves walked or rode (by horse, carriage, boat, or—in the case of Frederick Douglass— train), Henry Brown somehow decided that he could escape detection from his owner and slavery sympathizers by having himself "nailed inside a wooden crate and shipped via the Adams Express Company from slavery in Richmond, Virginia, to freedom in Philadelphia, Pennsylvania," as Richard Newman notes in the Introduction to this edition of Brown's extraordinarily rare 1851 narrative. Confined for twenty-seven hours, Brown's most unusual conduit to freedom consisted of a baize-lined wooden casketlike container, three feet long and two feet wide, held shut with five hickory loops, traversing a distance of 350 miles.

Brown's mode of escape, sui generis, was both ingenious and dangerous. As he puts it in his text, "the idea suddenly flashed upon my mind" that it was possible to shut "myself up" and be delivered to a safe address in "a free state . . . as dry goods." (How dry Brown may have been after twenty-seven hours of confinement in a wooden box three feet by two feet, no one was apparently willing to say at the time.) Brown's accomplice, a white man named Samuel A. Smith, would be arrested seven months later for attempting this same scheme with two other slaves, as was a free black man, James Caesar Anthony Smith, who also helped Brown and Samuel Smith to effect Brown's successful escape in March 1849. Samuel Smith was jailed. James Smith, who admitted having helped slaves escape since 1826, was paradoxically acquitted. (Brown's container, by the way, had been constructed by a black carpenter named John Mattaner.)

Richard Newman documents Brown's subsequent career as a successful abolitionist lecturer and author, both in the North and in England, where he fled after the passage of the Fugitive Slave Act of 1850, and where he published the second and third editions of his slave narrative and became increasingly controversial within the abolitionist movement. In fact, no less a stalwart of the abolition movement than Frederick Douglass himself criticized Brown publicly for unveiling his method of escape, implying that Brown had chosen to profit from his own ingenuity rather than share it with other slaves who could have possibly utilized a similar passage to freedom.

Douglass, who considered the anti-slavery movement the moral equivalent of war, declined in his slave narrative of 1845 to disclose his mode of escape, which was to assume the disguise of a sailor and ride a train from slavery in Baltimore to freedom in Philadelphia. It is highly unlikely, however, that other slaves were able to utilize Douglass's ruse, despite his discretion. Nonetheless, this contretemps between the two slave narrators who fled enslavement by rail is indicative of deep ambivalences within the abolitionist movement about disclosure and discretion and, indeed, about the entire profit-making aspect of the anti-slavery lecture circuit.

Henry Box Brown was a hugely popular lecturer; his story was so unusual, his method of escape so uncannily bold, that listeners and readers devoured his story, overcoming their skepticism about Brown's veracity by insisting that Brown reenact his escape mechanism, which he did in England.

The perennial appeal of Brown's tale to his contemporaries and to us, a century and a half later, stems, in part, from the fact that Brown made literal much that was implicit in the symbolism of enslavement. Slavery was a form of "social death," as the sociologist Orlando Patterson has famously discussed. The slave narratives were "narratives of ascent," as Robert Stepto has argued, stories of deliverance not only from slavery to freedom and South to North but also, in Patterson's sense, from social death to social life, even if a less than perfect life of a black person in the North of antebellum America. Brown *names* this symbolic relation between death and life by having himself confined in a virtual casket. He "descends" in what must have been a hellacious passage of the train ride—sweltering, suffocating, claustrophobic, unsanitary, devoid of light, food, and water—only to be resurrected twenty-seven hours later in the heavenly city of freedom and brotherly love that Philadelphia represented.

Brown, in other words, unwittingly had replicated the symbolic aspect of the crucifixion of Christ. He was the man who had been buried alive, yet lived to tell—and write—about it. Brown represented the potential of all slaves to return from the death-in-life that slavery was for the slave. Moreover, that it was a slave who devised this clever act of illusion—in clear defiance of racist claims that African slaves were pre-rational—only made Brown's echo of the most important element in the whole of Christian symbolism all the more compelling. Brown was a Christlike figure, an escape artist, and something of an inventor all rolled into one. His text resonated for readers on each of these deeper levels.

That a slave would risk death by suffocation or dehydration to gain his freedom, in defiance of all odds for his own survival, and that he used two symbols of the official power structure—a shipping firm and the railroad—to do so, not only astonished his readers, but calls to mind in our own generation the determination to achieve democracy by oppressed peoples throughout the world. Clearly, for Brown, the will to flight was paramount, just as it continues to be for refugees fleeing totalitarian regimes today, from Bosnia to Burundi, from Cuba to China, from Turkistany to Tibet. Henry Box Brown's story is just as relevant now as it was 150 years ago.

The scholar Richard Newman has performed a most outstanding and admirable service in restoring this rare and compelling text to a new generation of readers.

Introduction

by Richard Newman

The Book

O f the hundreds of thousands of African-American slaves who liberated themselves by escaping from human bondage in the South, very few specific names remain with us. Most, in fact, are not even known. Some ex-slaves, however, told or wrote the stories of their lives. These narratives give us much of what we know, not only about the resistance of escape, but about slave life and thought.

One name that has not been forgotten is Henry "Box" Brown. He is stamped indelibly on the popular imagination because of his ingenious method of escape. On March 29, 1849, Brown had himself nailed inside a wooden crate and shipped via the Adams Express Co. from slavery in Richmond, Virginia, to freedom in Philadelphia, Pennsylvania. In twenty-seven hours, he traveled 350 miles, most of it in discomfort and all of it in danger.

Brown, who immediately took the name "Box" as his own, has retained the public recognition he achieved at the time of his bold flight. A black wax museum in Baltimore features a life-size Brown emerging from his packing crate. The National Park Service recommends that its site guides relate Brown's unique tale as a way to humanize any discussion of slavery, a subject most tourists apparently resist. Toyota Motors Sales Co. recently ran an advertisement telling Brown's story, picturing a large box, and "recognizing those individuals who overcame great obstacles."

The fugitives we know are remembered primarily through their published narratives. Box Brown also issued an account of his life and escape, but his book is essentially unavailable. The first edition, published in Boston in 1849, the same year as his escape, is also highly flawed. Brown, like most other slaves, was illiterate, so his and their stories were told by sympathetic whites, more or less based on their subjects' verbal accounts. Brown's amanuensis, Charles Stearns, was perhaps the first white man to write a narrative on behalf of a slave. Stearns was such a zealous abolitionist, however, that Brown's story is spoiled by Stearns' turgid style, scolding prose, and even the addition of a polemic essay of his own. It is hardly Box Brown's book.

Fearful of capture because of the Fugitive Slave Act of 1850, Brown was forced to flee to England soon after his arrival in the North. In England, he, or someone under his direction, edited Stearns' overblown rhetoric out of the narrative, and a new version was issued in Manchester in 1851. The excision of Sterns' words and rhetoric is clear evidence of the kinds of restrictions ex-slaves faced under the control of their best anti-slavery white friends. Unable to read or write and with little access to printers or publishers, Box Brown was not free from saying what other people wanted him to say. Only in England did he experience the freedom to express himself in his own way. The Manchester editon is obviously closer to Brown's own telling of his own story, but it has never been published in the United States— until now.

The differences between the two books are clear from their titles. The American title is *Narrative of Henry Box Brown who Escaped from Slavery Enclosed in a Box 3 Feet Long and 2 Wide Written from a Statement of Facts*

Made by Himself. With Remarks upon the Remedy for Slavery. By Charles Stearns. This book, a reprinting of Brown's Manchester version, is simply entitled *Narrative of the Life of Henry Box Brown, Written by Himself* and is twenty-three pages shorter. The real difference is that this version is told in Brown's own voice.

In their original published forms, both these books are scarce. Philip McBlain, the leading dealer in rare African-American books, reports that he has never seen a copy of the American edition. The New York book dealer Glen Horowitz did offer one for sale in 1996 at $5,500. It does exist in major research libraries, however, and there were several reprints in the late 1960s, but now even these have disappeared. A dozen copies of this 1851 Manchester edition are in American libraries.

A second English edition came out in Bilston in 1852, but the stereotyped text is the same as this volume. The Bilston reprint indicates the book's popularity in the United Kingdom, where Brown became a feature on the abolitionist lecture circuit, as he had been in the United States. Currently, there is only one known copy of the 1852 edition in the United States.

Brown's Story

Box Brown's birthdate, like that of all slaves, is uncertain, but we know he was born on a plantation in Louisa County, Virginia, near the capital city of Richmond, sometime around 1815. The first half of the nineteenth century through which he lived was a momentous period for a nation struggling with the crisis of slavery. The very existence of the United States as a federal union was at stake, first when the moralistic New England abolitionists cried, "No union with slaveholders," then when the white South used states' rights as a rationalization to protect the slave system.

Brown lived through a time of increasing national polarization. In the years before he became a fugitive, the South toughened its position, particularly as it saw the western territories as potential ground for the addition of slave states. In 1816, the American Colonization Society was formed to eliminate the "danger" of free Negroes in a slave society by shipping them to Africa. In the 1830s, black literacy was forbidden by law in many states. In 1836, a gag rule forbade even the introduction of anti-slavery legislation in the U.S. Congress. When pro-slavery Missouri applied for statehood in 1818, Thomas Jefferson perceptively called it "a firebell in the night," an alarm and a warning that an inevitable conflagration lay ahead.

African Americans also strengthened their own resolve during Brown's lifetime. In 1827, the first black newspaper, *Freedom's Journal*, appeared in New York with the statement, "Too long have others spoken for us." Two years later, David Walker published in Boston his radical *Appeal*, calling for slave revolt. In 1831 Nat Turner in Virginia led the slaves' most successful rebellion. The famous *L'Amistad* mutiny was in 1839, and in 1843 Sojourner Truth became an anti-slavery activist. Personal escapes that came to national attention increased: Frederick Douglass in 1838, William and Ellen Craft in 1848, and Harriet Tubman just four months after Box Brown, in 1849.

The whole purpose of Brown's *Narrative* was, and continues to be, the creation of a medium for him to tell his own story. He describes his family and childhood, his work in a tobacco factory, and the heartbreaking account of the sale of his wife and children, which meant their forced separation. It was then that this law-abiding man decided to escape, and "the idea suddenly flashed upon my mind of shutting myself up in a box and getting myself conveyed as dry goods to a free State."

What did the slaves themselves, particularly the vast majority who were the plantation field hands, say was the worst aspect of bondage? It was not the whippings, the labor of sixteen-hour workdays, the food minimized to survival levels, the special clothing woven from mill-floor scraps. Their deepest anxiety and greatest suffering came from the arbitrary breaking up of their families, husbands from wives, parents from children, children from each other. This severance and sundering created an emotional death that left scars deeper than the lash marks on their backs.

Brown's five-foot, eight-inch, 200-pound body was fitted into a baize-lined container sealed by five hickory loops, marked "THIS SIDE UP WITH CARE," and mailed to William H. Johnson, an abolitionist sympathizer on Philadelphia's Arch Street. The city's Anti-Slavery Committee sent for the box, and it was brought to their office at 107 N. 5th Street on March 30, 1849. Nervous abolitionists opened the box, Henry Brown calmly emerged, said, "How do you do, gentlemen?" and promptly fainted.

After a glass of water, a disheveled Brown regained his aplomb and proceeded to sing the Fortieth Psalm. Provided with money and clothes, Brown stayed with abolitionists James and Lucretia Mott, and then was sent to Boston and New Bedford. Brown's imaginative escape immediately caught public attention. He became an instant celebrity, a status he discovered he liked and learned to exploit. He went on the abolitionist lecture circuit, singing his songs and telling his story.

Sentiment against slavery was rising in the North, largely because a national government dominated by pro-slavery southerners was pushing its agenda. Brown, and others, found increasingly sympathetic audiences. Northern whites were particularly attracted to fugitive slaves who could describe from their own experiences what slavery was really like. They were fascinated by Brown, in part, of course, because of his successful but dangerous escape. He stayed on tour until the early fall of 1850.

The Smiths

Back in Virginia, meanwhile, the seriousness of Brown's escape was dramatized by the arrest of Samuel A. Smith, the white man who facilitated

Brown's flight by packing him into his famous box. Smith was convicted in October 1849 for boxing up two more potential escapees, Alfred and Sawney, who were discovered and captured. Smith was refused witnesses, and spent five summer months chained in a cell five feet by eight feet, not unlike the restrained enclosure of his friend Brown. In prison, Smith survived five stab wounds, reportedly inflicted by a hired assassin. Like St. Paul, however, Smith converted his jailer—who petitioned the governor of Virginia for Smith's release. The governor refused, and Smith was not set free until June 18, 1856.

James Caesar Anthony Smith, the free black who helped Samuel Smith ship Brown to Philadelphia, was also arrested and tried. He allegedly introduced Alfred and Sawney to Samuel Smith, and he was therefore charged as an accomplice in the conspiracy to assist their escape. J. C. A. Smith also allegedly outfitted escape trunks that had been constructed by John Mattauer, a black carpenter. Smith admitted having helped slaves escape since 1826. Interestingly, while the white Samuel Smith was convicted, the black J. C. A. Smith was released, perhaps because a lawyer who charged $900 argued his case.

Immediately following his release, Samuel A. Smith left the South for Philadelphia, the same destination as Brown. Well aware of his role in Brown's escape as well as Smith's own personal suffering, Philadelphia's African-American community held a mass meeting on his behalf at the Israel Church on July 1, 1856. After hearing Smith quietly recount his experience in prison, the meeting passed this resolution:

> We the colored citizens of Philadelphia, have among us Samuel A. Smith, who was incarcerated over seven years in Richmond Penitentiary, for doing an act that was honorable to his feelings and his sense of justice and humanity, therefore.
>
> Resolved, That we welcome him to this city as a martyr to the cause of Freedom.

Resolved, That we heartily tender him our gratitude for the good he has done to our suffering race.

Resistance

Although history has long recognized white abolitionists, it has largely ignored the anti-slavery struggle of African Americans, even though it was the blacks themselves who were the real abolitionists. The people who were against slavery were, after all, the slaves. There were 3,204,313 slaves in the United States in 1850, owned by 347,725 white families. Slave resistance to bondage started at the plantation itself: slowed-down work, theft, broken tools, stable doors left open, crops damaged, dissembling, feigned illnesses. There was a second level: burned barns and poisoned soup. And a third: armed rebellion. At least 250 slave revolts in the United States have been documented, and recent research on the Atlantic slave trade documents another 250 aboard ship.

In the North, free blacks supported their brothers and sisters in chains. Most opposed the American Colonization Society, and strengthened their resolve to achieve black freedom in this country. African Americans organized themselves against slavery, petitioned, founded newspapers, held mass meetings, and even urged slave rebellion. There were over fifty black anti-slavery societies by 1830, all before William Lloyd Garrison formed the American Anti-Slavery Society in 1833. Garrison's famous *Liberator* newspaper was subsidized and subscribed to by people of color.

The major resistance to slavery, however, was escape, what Frederick Douglass called "praying with your feet." With his unique variation, this was the means Box Brown chose to free himself. Running away was by definition a secret and dangerous undertaking, not only illegal, but with high prices to pay by those who were captured. As a result, many aspects and elements of the process are not now fully known.

Many runaways followed the North Star to the free states and Canada, but a large number, almost entirely undocumented, escaped to Mexico, where they disappeared into the population. The estimate is that several thousand slaves became fugitives from the South's "peculiar institution" each year during the first half of the nineteenth century.

It was not death, but life, not heaven, but Canada that was the encoded message of the slave song:

No more auction block for me,
No more, no more.
No more auction block for me,
Many thousand gone.

While many fugitives made their way on their own, others followed the Underground Railroad, a loose network of clandestine escape routes. There were signals, disguises, passwords, safe houses, and guides or "conductors." With a price on her head, Harriet Tubman made repeated trips below the Mason-Dixon line to bring out men, women, and children. Fugitives traveled by boat and wagon, but mostly by foot, often walking at night and hiding during the day, but always heading North. Since slaves were legally defined as property, escape was actually a curious form of the slaves' stealing themselves.

We are just now discovering some of the hidden aspects of escape. African-American-made quilts, for example, innocently airing in a cabin window, were sometimes disguised maps, and could contain coded messages about dangers and directions. It is now well-known that the slave songs or Negro Spirituals are full of allusions to escape as well as ways of communicating within the black community without white people understanding what was being said. In these songs, for example, Canaan is Canada; the Jordan is the Ohio River (the dividing line between the slave and free states); and the many references to travel (shoes, wheels, chariots, trains) are all about running away.

Slave Narratives

In 1849, the year of Brown's escape, Ephriam Peabody, the minister of Boston's King's Chapel, commented that America had contributed a new genre to world literature—the slave narrative. Nineteenth-century America was a land dominated by slavery in economics, politics, and social relationships, and where nearly every African American was in bondage. It is not until we hear the voices of these slaves themselves, therefore, that we can begin to understand who the vast number of African Americans were and what their lives, thoughts, and experiences were all about.

It is not known how many ex-slaves told their stories in published form, but there were many hundreds—in books, pamphlets, newspapers, magazines, every medium of the day. It is generally held that *A Narrative of the Unknown Sufferings and Surprising Deliverance of Briton Hammon, a Negro Man* issued in 1760 was the first, and that this distinctive category of American literature concludes with Booker T. Washington's 1901 autobiographical classic *Up from Slavery*. Slave narratives in fact constitute the basis of the African-American literary tradition. Early writers like Phillis Wheatley largely reflect European style and content.

Box Brown's *Narrative* shares several characteristics typical of the genre. It follows the usual outline of events. It serves as an anti-slavery tract. It is a way to make money, the purpose of which was often to help ex-slaves buy their wives and children still in bondage. Brown's narrative advertises his abolitionist lectures and is a memento to be sold afterwards. Brown took very easily to his new role as author and lecturer, and the income provided his livelihood.

In examining these narratives, credibility is often in question. Ulrich B. Phillips, whose right-wing views dominated the historiography of slavery virtually until the modern Civil Rights Movement, insisted that slave narratives were unreliable. A few are, in fact, novels or novelized. There is considerable external evidence, it should be said, to confirm completely Box Brown's account of his life.

Some slave autobiographies were careful, reluctant, or even silent with some facts because it would have been dangerous to expose names and places involved in their escapes. In his later autobiographies, Frederick Douglass not only reveals more information about his own flight, he admonishes Brown for "drawing attention to the manner of his escape," and bluntly claims that, if he had not, "we might have had a thousand Box Browns per annum."

But something far more important is going on here. The literary critic Henry Louis Gates, Jr. points out that "the act of writing for the slave constituted an act of creating a public, historical self." That is, those who were defined by law and custom as less than human literally wrote themselves into human existence as men and women. Denied both a meaningful history and a status within humanity, slave autobiographies, even when composed by others, made it possible for African Americans to become the sources of their own history and the authenticators of their own existence.

The self-creation of autobiography obviously follows the self-liberation of escape. Gates suggests that white people usually write their biographies at the conclusion of their careers, while blacks tend to begin their careers with autobiographies—in order to establish and confirm themselves at the outset as real and visible selves in America's racist society. They may now be unknown or forgotten, but, as Vijayalakshumi Teclock points out, every slave had a face and a name, a story to relate, a past and a future. To see that name in print goes beyond validation to a kind of human triumph.

Slave narratives constitute, therefore, a literature of resistance and a means of subversion at the same time that they are personal memoirs and historical documents. These are themes that continue in African-American literature in such autobiographies as those of Malcolm X, Anne Moody, and the series of memoirs by Maya Angelou. The motifs even spill over into fiction, in such biographical-type novels as Richard Wright's *Native Son*, Ralph Ellison's *Invisible Man*, and Toni Morrison's *Beloved*.

Charles Stearns

Who was the man who first wrote and published Box Brown's narrative? He was obviously personally inspired by Brown, and, even more so, saw the propaganda uses to which Brown's story could be put. Charles B. Stearns (1818–1899) was a doctrinaire pacifist, a militant Garrisonian abolitionist, and an activist participant during Reconstruction in schemes to reform southern plantation agriculture. Born in Greenfield, Massachusetts, Stearns may have inherited his radicalism from his mother's brother, George Ripley, the founder of the utopian colony Brook Farm.

Oberlin College reports Stearns' attending their preparatory school in 1841–1842. Influenced by the evangelist Charles Finney, he intended to study for the ministry. Early on, Stearns became an argumentative ideologue who embraced pacifism and vehemently denounced all physical force. In 1845, he instigated the curious "Rights of God" controversy in the pages of Garrison's *Liberator*. He legalistically argued that the biblical God who takes human life and punishes sinners runs contrary to God's own self-imposed limitations, and so even God himself has no right to kill.

In the 1850s, the struggle over the admission of Kansas into the union as a free or slave state inspired many white New England abolitionists to migrate, especially to the city of Lawrence, the center of free state agitation. Stearns opened a store there while he served as a correspondent for the *Liberator* and the *National Anti-Slavery Standard*. On May 1, 1856, pro-slavery forces from Missouri attacked Lawrence. Stearns' store was sacked and burned, his clerk was murdered, and he barely escaped with his life.

The violence of pro-slavery "Border Ruffians" in Bleeding Kansas utterly demolished Stearns' doctrinaire pacifism, and, perhaps because he was a natural extremist, pushed him to the totally opposite end of the spectrum. "When I live with men made in God's image, I will never shoot them," Stearns wrote to the *Milford* [MA] *Practical Christian* in 1856, "but these pro-slavery Missourians are demons from the bottomless pit and may be shot with impunity." Pacifist and abolitionist Abby Kelly Foster admitted, somewhat more mildly, that "Kansas was the great argument against us."

Following the Civil War, Stearns and his wife bought a plantation in Columbia County, Georgia, apparently to participate in land reform during Reconstruction. Stearns was involved with the Laborers' Homestead and Southern Emancipation Society of which his fellow Garrisonian James Buffam was director. In 1869, Stearns sold the plantation and moved to Boston. Here his trail runs cold, but this acerbic and difficult man deserves a biography, if for no other reason than that he gave us Brown's.

Deliverance

As Henry Brown emerged from the packing crate, his first act as a liberated man was to sing the Fortieth Psalm. This was obviously an intentional and carefully planned performance on Brown's part to which he must have given much thought. The psalm continued to be important enough to Brown for him to include the text in both the American and British versions of his autobiography. It also became part of his stage presentations in this country and abroad.

In biblically literate Protestant America, especially the evangelical South, Brown would have been intimately familiar with the Psalter. The words he chose are strikingly appropriate to him and his situation. Psalm 40 actually consists of two separate songs: verses 1–11 and verses 13–17. Brown sings, in anthem form, the first song. It is a public pronouncement of righteousness; it is "the glad news of deliverance," as the Revised Standard Version translates it. The singer praises God: "I waited patiently for the Lord; and . . . he heard my cry." God has brought the singer up "out of a horrible pit" and "out of the miry clay," synonyms for hell, and "set my feet upon a rock."

This long-awaited and miraculous deliverance calls for "a new song" that "many shall see," and, as a consequence, "trust in the Lord." Brown fulfills this prophecy by his performance in the Anti-Slavery Office and on stage. Brown's new song stands in fulfillment, also, of a newspaper report at the time of Brown's escape explaining what and why he had done: "After his wife and children were stolen, his heart was broken. He had learned to sing, to lighten the tedium of his labor, and for the gratification of his fellow captives, but now he could not sing."

The psalm perfectly describes Brown's own personal experience. He can affirm, "Thou art my help and my deliverer," or, in the New World Translation, "You are my assistance and the provider of escape for me." For Brown the evangelical Christian, this is all not a matter of locating relevant verses about deliverance and escape, nor even of believing that the Bible somehow engages him personally, but, rather, of understanding that the Bible at its deepest level tells his own existential story.

Uncle Ned

Having discovered the pleasures and power of performance, Brown adapted the lyrics of a popular song of the day into another medium for him to tell his story. The song was "Uncle Ned," sometimes called "Old Uncle Ned," composed by Stephen Foster (1826–1864), and Brown made the rewritten version part of his own repertoire.

Foster's original "Uncle Ned" was one of the earliest songs by the man who would become "America's Troubadour," the composer of some of the country's most familiar and popular ballads, from "Oh Susanna" and "Camptown Races" to "Way Down upon the Suwanee River." Foster wrote "Uncle Ned" in 1848, the year before Brown's escape:

> Dere was an old Nigga, dey called him Uncle Ned —
> He's dead long ago, long ago!
> He had no wool on de top ob his head —
> De place whar de wool ought to grow.

Chorus

> Den lay down de shubble and de hoe,
> Hang up de fiddle and de bow;
> No more hard work for poor Old Ned —
> He is gone whar de good Niggas go.

> His fingers were long like de cane in de brake,
> He had no eyes for to see,
> He had no teeth for to eat de corn cake
> So he had to let de corn cake be.

> When Old Ned die, Massa take it mighty bad,
> De tears run down like de rain,
> Old Missus turn pale and she get berry sad,

Cayse she nebber see Old Ned again.

The racism of "Uncle Ned" is obvious, with its dialect, "Niggas," and old Massa and pale Missus' tears at the demise of their human property. Foster's defenders, however, claim that the song compassionately sympathizes with the dead slave, however romantic and sentimentalized the depiction of the mythical South. There is undoubtedly, it must be said, an element of black folk balladry in all of Foster's songs. The African-American philosopher Alain Locke even suggests that Foster shares the same relation to Negro folk songs as Joel Chandler Harris does to Negro folktales. That is, a tradition is preserved and distorted at the same time, perhaps a necessary condition for that tradition to enter mainstream (i.e., white) culture.

Foster certainly was exposed early to vernacular black culture. He lived during this period of his life in Cincinnati, just across the Ohio River from the slavocracy. His family's black servant, Olivia Pise, took him to black church meetings, he often visited the slave state of Kentucky, and he heard the singing of black stevedores who labored near his own workplace. Foster undoubtedly absorbed and exploited this tradition.

"Uncle Ned" became an immediate hit in America and abroad. The Foster Hall Collection at the University of Pittsburgh reports fifty-three different editions printed in 1848 alone. As "An Ethiopian Melody," it became a standard feature of minstrel shows, where black-based music, dance, humor, and style were appropriated by white people who turned them into racist entertainment. Brown simply but decisively reversed the process when his version transformed "Uncle Ned" into a celebration of his freedom.

All the verses of Brown's subversive adaptation, what scholars of African American literature might call "signifying," are in his text, but it begins:

Have you seen a man by the name of Henry Brown,
Ran away from the South to the North;
Which he would not have done but they stole all his rights,
But they'll never do the like again.
Chorus
Brown laid down the shovel and the hoe,
Down in the box he did go;
No more slave work for Henry Box Brown,
In the box by express he did go.

Brown was not alone in subverting "Uncle Ned" via new lyrics. In his
serialized 1850s novel *Blake*, Martin Delany includes another version:

Hang up the shovel and the hoe-o-o-o!
I don't care whether I work or no!
Old master's gone to the slaveholder's rest
He's gone where they all ought to go.

The Panorama

Success as a speaker and singer performing on the anti-slavery circuit
not only agreed with Brown, it encouraged his abilities as an entrepre-
neur. The imagination that led him in the first place to his box now
blossomed into an idea for a massive and spectacular panorama, a pic-
torial representation exhibited with changing scenes. A panorama as
such was not an original idea of Brown's, but he grasped its potential
significance both as a way to communicate the story of slavery through
revealing comprehensible images, as well as to appeal to a public
always receptive to something new and different.

On February 1, 1850, Brown wrote Gerrit Smith, the wealthy white
abolitionist, and asked for a loan of $150 to pay for his panorama.

Brown engaged Josiah Wolcott to design and paint it, perhaps with the assistance of other artists. Wolcott was a white painter of portraits and of New England natural scenes in the Hudson River School style. One of his better known works is of Brook Farm, the utopian community in West Roxbury, Massachusetts. Brown's panorama was entitled *The Mirror of Slavery*. It is now lost, but it certainly consisted of many thousands of square feet of canvas.

Brown made a second inspired choice in recruiting Benjamin F. Roberts to prepare an accompanying text and lecture, "The Condition of the Colored People in the United States." Roberts was an African-American Boston printer who, the year before, had filed a suit for the integration of Boston's public schools on behalf of his daughter Sarah, but the state Supreme Court ruled in favor of the city. Roberts also represented "A Committee of Colored Gentlemen" who had reissued in 1844 R. B. Lewis's *Light and Truth*, one of the first histories of people of color by an African American.

The *Mirror of Slavery* opened to the public on April 19, 1850, in Washington Hall on Boston's Bromfield Street. Admission was twenty-five cents for adults, with children at half-price. The panorama was exhibited for several months, and then it traveled to other New England towns in a tour coordinated by Roberts. When Brown fled the country in September, he managed to transport *The Mirror of Slavery* to England. Now accompanied by J. C. A. Smith, Brown put *The Mirror of Slavery* back on the road until the men split up and each went his separate way.

The Mirror of Slavery was not only a presentation by people of color, it portrayed images and views of American history as people of color perceived that history. The panorama of some fifty pictures opened with the beginning of it all, *The African Slave Trade*, the centuries old human commerce that had devastated Africa and corrupted America. The second and third images, *The Nubian Family in Freedom* and *The Seizure of Slaves*, revealed the destruction of the Old World; they were followed by *The Nubian Family at Auction* and *Modes of Confinement and Punishment* that revealed the depravity of the New World.

Brown aptly alternated traditional American scenic views, like *View of Richmond, Va.* with such scenes as *Whipping Post and Gallows at Richmond, Va.* He did the same with *Washington's Tomb at Mount Vernon* and *Slave Prisons at Washington.* This interspersion threw into question every conventional idea of the American landscape. Just as Brown's version of "Uncle Ned" turned a sentimental ballad into a protest song, so his picture of America transformed sentimental representations into an honest reality most white Americans had never seen. Not to minimize his own historical role, Brown included two images of his own escape.

England

The Compromise of 1850 was another futile attempt to hold together an America deeply fractured over the issue of slavery. For African Americans and their white abolitionist friends, the most objectionable feature of the Compromise was its strengthened Fugitive Slave Act. Now federal law required free people in the North to aid in the capture and return of black runaways. The law was often met with noncompliance and even resistance. On August 30, 1850, Henry Box Brown narrowly escaped capture by slave agents in Providence, Rhode Island. So did his tour companion, J. C. A. Smith, even though he was a freeborn Negro.

Both men fled to England, arriving in Liverpool in late October. Brown lectured, sold lithographs of himself, and sang spirituals, antislavery songs, and hymns to raise money for the shipment of his panorama. With *The Mirror of Slavery* Brown and Smith toured the north of England in the winter and spring of 1850–1851. Brown's showmanship developed even further, and he had himself shipped, theatrically, in his famous box from Bradford to Leeds.

Friction, probably over money, developed between Brown and Smith, and Brown officially dissolved their partnership on July 25, 1851. Now both men traveled the U.K. lecture circuit, each with his own panorama. We next get a picture of a new and different Brown, but it is hardly an unbiased view since it comes from the spurned J. C. A. Smith. On August 6 from Manchester, Smith wrote Gerrit Smith to complain about Brown's breaking up their partnership and allegedly taking the money.

"Brown has behaved very bad sense he have been here," Smith asserted, citing Brown's drinking, smoking, gambling, swearing, and said he "do many other things too Bad—to think off." What could be too bad to think of? "He have got it to his head to get a wife or something *worst*." Smith claimed Brown could have purchased his enslaved wife and children from their American bondage, but that he was apparently being seduced into the fast life of England. What was the evidence?

Smith said Brown was drinking "Rasbury wine, pop, pepermint, Sampson, ginger Beer, gingerale, Blackbeer . . . and many other things of that nature," although he admitted none of these beverages was actually alcoholic. Brown was also "smoking pipe, segars, and chewing tobacco, takin' snuff," as well as swearing. The gambling consisted of "playing doman noes-dice, drafts, and Be[g]ertels." These may seem like innocent pastimes, but they were intended to discredit Brown by being reported to the pietistic and moralistic white American abolitionist community.

What happened to Brown is as yet unknown. Various unsubstantiated rumors have him adding minstrelsy to his performance, marrying an Englishwoman, and disappearing into Wales. No one has made a concerted effort to track Brown at this point, but there must be newspapers and civic records that could complete his story. Brown began and spent most of his life in anonymity, and, at least so far as we now know, ended it the same way.

The Allegorical Box

The basic notion of a person emerging from a confined space is a deceptively simple one. The obvious analogy is the dead rising up from their coffins and graves. Indeed, the literature and images of his day spoke often of Brown's resurrection. To an evangelically attuned society, white and black, the physical resurrection of the body was an entirely familiar and real expectation, as was the transformation from death in this world to new life in the next. As a metaphor, Brown's image resonated easily, familiarly, and unambiguously on the evangelical eye and ear, and, through them, on the American imagination.

There is a second major trope in Brown's confinement and emergence, but one that he transformed to the point of reversal. The Middle Passage was the most horrendous and torturous aspect of the Atlantic slave trade. Unmercifully packed together in sailing ships, Africans were pressed into enclosures little more than living tombs. With slaves defined as nonhuman products for the commodity market, they were crammed into spaces designed only to maximize numbers and profits. The result was hell.

Sickness, whipping, dysentery, and suicide turned slave ships' holds into slaughterhouses where the stench of blood and flux could be smelled as far as five miles away across the open sea. In this way, over the centuries, more than 15 million men, women, and children experienced their transport from African freedom to American slavery and were introduced to the horrors of the New World. Cynthia Griffin Wolff writes tellingly of Brown within this context: "He would transform this [Middle Passage] text into its opposite by converting the very stringencies of an African slave ship into a blueprint for freedom."

When one thinks about it, the box as container and symbol turns up everywhere. In Brown's own escape year of 1849 Rose Jackson, an Oklahoma slave who chose to stay with her owners on their trek west, was smuggled in a box over the whole length of the Oregon Trail, since slaves were forbidden in the Territory. During the Civil War, South Carolina slaves Anne and William Summerson were hidden in rice casks and successfully brought to the Charleston docks. William Still's history of the Underground Railroad in Philadelphia reports a number of ingenious escapes, including what he called "other box or chest cases."

In 1996, Anthony Cohen, who retraces the journeys of escaped slaves, reenacted Brown's ordeal by having himself shipped over seven hours by train from Philadelphia to New York. Two years later he spent sixteen hours in a crate on the Memphis to Chicago Amtrak. Speaking of Amtrak, there is on the Internet a satire of Amtrak describing "Amtrek Econobox Class," which promises "You'll love curling up in our compact wooden crate." The parody is accompanied, of course, by a drawing of Henry Box Brown.

A recent (and one of the more significant) legacy of Box Brown is Charles Burnett's film *The Final Insult* (1997). Recipient of a MacArthur "genius" grant, Burnett is probably best known for his award-winning *To Sleep with Anger* (1990), and he is widely considered one of the finest African-American writer-directors. The central character in *The Final Insult* is Box Brown, named by his mother for the fugitive slave. Burnett's Brown lives in today's Los Angeles, a city deteriorating with racism, deep class divisions, and increasingly severe economic disparities.

Brown loses his job in a Kafkaesque experience and is reduced to living in his boxlike automobile. His consuming hope is that he will not be reduced further yet, that is, forced to abandon his car to live, like many of his fellows, out of a shopping cart. This would be "the final insult." Of course, in this bitterly paradoxical story, that is precisely what happens. In an ironic twist on Box Brown's slave narrative, Burnett's Box Brown's container is not only his assurance of freedom, it is his freedom itself.

Brown's Legacy

Brown's life and work personify several of the interconnected themes integral to African-American experience and culture. First, he reinvents himself. Once a slave, he becomes free; once a factory worker, he becomes an abolitionist lecturer, writer, and performer; once a nonentity, he becomes somebody. He even changes his name to mark the defining event in his life and signify his new identity. In Britain, if his critic is to be believed, he transposes himself still further, from a humble, religious abolitionist to something of a worldly dandy.

Second, Brown improvises, personally incorporating the essence of black speech, style, and music. His box is an original method of self-liberation. His rewriting of "Uncle Ned" is more than a mere revision or adaptation; it is a trope that turns Uncle Ned upside down and on his head; the mythic and passive slave becomes the real and active freeman. Brown's performance keeps adding new riffs, from songs and a massive panorama, to perhaps even elements of minstrelsy. The reinvented Brown finds that the black cultural tradition of improvisation is, in truth, his way to meet, live, and prevail in his new life.

Literary critic Houston A. Baker points out that every African American serves a prison sentence—enslaved on plantations, segregated into ghettos, incarcerated in prisons and housing projects, trapped in ignorance and poverty, constrained in a box of one kind or another. It is precisely this imprisonment Henry Box Brown confronts, challenges, and defeats. Brown's final word and continuing message is that he used confinement to achieve his liberation.

RICHARD NEWMAN

Bibliography

Austin, Allan. D. "More Black Panoramas: An Addendum." *The Massachusetts Review* 37:4 (Winter 1996/1997), 636–639.

Blassingame, John W. *Slave Testimony: Two Centuries of Letters, Speeches, Interviews, and Autobiographies.* Baton Rouge: Louisiana State University Press, 1977.

Brooks, Daphne A. "The Escape Artist: Henry 'Box' Brown, Black Abolitionist Performance, and Moving Panoramas in Transatlantic Culture." Paper, American Studies Association, Washington, D.C., November 9, 2001.

Davis, Charles T. and Henry Louis Gates, Jr., eds. *The Slave's Narrative.* New York: Oxford University Press, 1985.

Gates, Henry Louis, Jr. *Figures in Black: Words, Signs, and the Racial Self.* New York: Oxford University Press, 1987.

Gunkel, Hermann. *The Psalms: A Form-Critical Introduction.* Philadelphia: Fortress Press, 1967.

Nichols, Charles H. *Many Thousand Gone: The Ex-Slaves' Account of Their Bondage and Freedom.* Leiden: E. J. Brill, 1963.

Ripley, C. Peter, ed. *The Black Abolitionist Papers.* Vol. 1, *The British Isles, 1830–1865.* Chapel Hill: University of North Carolina Press, 1985.

Still, William. *The Underground Railroad.* Philadelphia: Porter & Coates, 1872.

Van Wagenen, Avis S. *Genealogy and Memoirs of Charles and Nathaniel Stearns and Their Descendents.* Syracuse: Courier Printing Co., 1901.

Wood, Marcus. "'All right!' The Narrative of Henry Box Brown as a Test Case for the Racial Prescription of Rhetoric and Semiotics." *Proceedings of the American Antiquarian Society* 107:1 (1998), 65–104.

Woolf, Cynthia Griffin. "Passing Beyond the Middle Passage: Henry 'Box' Brown's Translations of Slavery." *The Massachusetts Review* 37:1 (Spring 1996), 23–44.

Henry Brown emerges from his box. The black man is William Still, conductor of Philadelphia's Underground Railroad.

Courtesy, American Antiquarian Society.

HENRY BOX BROWN.

The following remarkable incident exhibits the cruelty of the slave system, while it shows the ingenuity and desperate determination of its victims to escape from it :—

A few months ago, a slave in a Southern city managed to open a correspondence with a gentleman in a Northern city, with a view to effect his escape from bondage. Having arranged the preliminaries, he paid somebody $40 to box him up, and mark him, "This side up, with care," and take him to the Express office, consigned to his friend at the North. On the passage, being on board of a steamboat, he was accidentally turned head downward, and almost died with the rush of blood to the head. At the next change of transportation, however, he was turned right side up again; and after twenty-six hours' confinement arrived safely at his destination. On receiving the box, the gentleman had doubts whether he should find a corpse or a living man. He rapped lightly on the box, with the question, "All right!" and was delighted to hear the response, "All right, sir." The poor fellow was immediately liberated from his place of burial.

An engraving from *The Liberty Almanac*. William Still is not pictured.

Courtesy, American Antiquarian Society.

This 1849 broadside contains the full text of Brown's parody of "Uncle Ned." Brown probably sold copies at his lectures.

Courtesy, American Antiquarian Society.

Engraving of the Box in which HENRY BOX
BROWN escaped from slavery in Richmond, Va.

A Boston engraving of the text of the 40th Psalm. Singing this song was
Brown's first act as a free person.

Courtesy, American Antiquarian Society.

This image was used to advertise Brown's book, but it also appeared on the cover of an 1854 book on the famous runaway Anthony Burns.

Author's collection.

HENRY BOX BROWN.

I will tell you the story of Henry Box
Brown. It is a strange tale, and it is all true.
Henry was a slave in Richmond, Virginia, and
then his name was Henry Brown. He had a
wife and four little children whom he loved
very much.

One night when he went home to his little
hut, his children and their mother, were gone,
and poor Henry found they had been sold to
a trader, and were taken away to Carolina. It
made him almost crazy to hear this dreadful

An illustration from an 1849 book of children's stories.

Courtesy, American Antiquarian Society.

PREFACE

by Henry Box Brown

So much has already been written concerning the evils of slavery, and by men so much more able to portray its horrid form
than I am, that I might well be excused if I were to remain altogether silent on the subject; but however much has been written,
however much has been said, and however much has been done, I
feel impelled by the voice of my own conscience, from the recent
experience which I have had of the alarming extent to which the
traffic in human beings is carried on, and the cruelties, both bodily
and mental, to which men in the condition of slaves are continually
subjected, and also from the hardening and blasting influences
which this traffic produces on the character of those who thus treat
as goods and chattels the bodies and souls of their fellows, to add
yet one other testimony of, and protest against, the foul blot on
the state of morals, of religion, and of cultivation in the American
republic. For I feel convinced that enough has not been written,
enough has not been said, enough has not been done, while nearly
four millions of human beings, possessing immortal souls, are, in
chains, dragging out their existence in the southern states. They

3

are keenly alive to the heaven born voice of liberty, and require the illumination of the grace of Almighty God. Having, myself, been in that same position, but by the blessing of God having been enabled to snap my chains and escape to a land of liberty—I owe it as a sacred duty to the cause of humanity, that I should devote my life to the redemption of my fellow men.

The tale of my own sufferings is not one of great interest to those who delight to read of hair-breadth adventures, of tragic occurrences, and scenes of blood—my life, even in slavery, has been in many respects comparatively comfortable. I have experienced a continuance of such kindness, as slaveholders have to bestow; but though my body has escaped the lash of the whip, my mind has groaned under tortures which I believe will never be related, because, language is inadequate to express them, but those know them who have them to endure. The whip, the cowskin, the gallows, the stocks, the paddle, the prison, the perversion of the stomach—although bloody and barbarous in their nature—have no comparison with those internal pangs which are felt by the soul when the hand of the merciless tyrant plucks from one's bosom the object of one's ripened affections, and the darlings who in requiring parental care, confer the sweet sensations of parental bliss. I freely admit I have enjoyed my full share of all those blessings which fall to the lot of a slave's existence. I have felt the sweet influence of friendships' power, and the still more delightful glow of love; and had I never heard the name of liberty or seen the tyrant lift his cruel hand to smite my fellow and my friend, I might perhaps have dragged my chains in quietude to the grave, and have found a tomb in a slavery-polluted land; but thanks be to God I heard the glorious sound and felt its inspiring influence on my heart, and having satisfied myself of the value of freedom. I resolved to purchase it whatever should be its price.

INTRODUCTION

by Henry Box Brown

While America is boasting of her freedom and making the world ring with her professions of equality, she holds millions of her inhabitants in bondage. This surely must be a wonder to all who seriously reflect on the subject of man holding property in man, in a land of republican institutions. That slavery, in all its phases, is demoralizing to every one concerned, none who may read the following narrative, can for a moment doubt. In my opinion unless the Americans purge themselves of this stain, they will have to undergo very severe, if not protracted suffering. It is not at all unlikely that the great unsettledness which of late has attached to the prices of cotton; the very unsatisfactory circumstance of that slaveholding continent being the principal field employed in the production of that vegetable, by the dealing in, and the manufacture of, which, such astonishing fortunes have been amassed—will lead to arrangements being entered into, through the operation of which the bondmen will be made free. The popular mind is, in every land becoming impatient of its chains; and soon the American captives will be made to taste of that freedom, which by right, belongs to man. The manner in which this mighty change will be accomplished, may *not* be at present understood, but with the Lord all things are possible. It may be, that the very means which are being used by those who wish to perpetuate slavery, and to recapture those who have by any plans not approved of by those dealers in human flesh, become free, will be amongst the instruments which God will employ to overturn the whole system.

Another means which, in addition to the above, we think, will contribute to the accomplishment of this desirable object—the destruction of slavery—is the simple, but natural narrations of those who have been long under the yoke themselves. It is a lamentable fact that some ministers of religion are contaminated with the foulness of slavery. Those men, in the southern states, who ascend the pulpit to proclaim the world's jubilee, are themselves, in fearful numbers, the holders of slaves! When we reflect on the bar which slavery constituted to the advancement of the objects at one time contemplated by the almost defunct "Evangelical Alliance"; when we consider that Great Being who beheld the Israelites in their captivity, and beholding, came down to deliver them is still the same; have we not reason to believe that he will in his Providence raise up another Moses, to guide the now enslaved sons of Ham to the privileges which humanity, irrespective of colour or clime, is always at liberty to demand. While the British mind retains its antipathy to slavery in all its kinds, and sends forth its waves of audibly expressed opinion on the subject, that opinion, meeting with one nearly allied in character to itself in the Northern States; and while both unite in tending towards the South the reiterated demand for an honest acting, one those turgid profession of equality peculiar to all American proceedings—in every thing but slavery—the Southern states must yield to the pressure from without; even the slaves will feel themselves growing beyond the dimensions which their chains can enclose, and backed by the roar of the British Lion, and supported by Northern Americans in their just demand for emancipation, the long downtrodden and despised bondmen will arise, and by a united voice assert their title to freedom. It may be that the subject of the following narrative has a mission from God to the human family. Certainly the deliverance of Moses, from destruction on the Nile, was scarcely more marvellous than was the deliverance of Mr. Henry Box Brown from the horrors of slavery. For any lengthy observations, by which the reader will be detained from the subject of the following pages, there can be no necessity whatever.

Mr. Brown was conveyed from Richmond, Virginia, to Philadelphia in a box, three feet long, and two feet six inches deep. For twenty-seven hours he was enclosed in this box. The following copy of a letter which was written by the gentleman to whom it was directed, will explain this part of the subject:—

Copy of a Letter respecting Henry Box Brown's escape from Slavery— a verification of Patrick Henry's Speech in Virginia Legislature, March, 1775, when he said, *"Give me Liberty or give me Death."*

Philadelphia, March 26th, 1849.

DEAR—

Here is a man who has been the hero of one of the most extraordinary achievements I ever heard of;—he came to me on Saturday Morning last, in a box tightly hooped, marked "THIS SIDE UP," by *overland express, from the city of Richmond!!* Did you ever hear of any thing in all your life to beat that? Nothing that was done on the barricades of Paris exceeded this cool and deliberate intrepidity. To appreciate fully the boldness and risk of the achievement, you ought to see the box and hear all the circumstances. The box is in the clear three feet one inch long, two feet six inches deep, and two feet wide. It was a regular old store box, such as you see in Pearl street;—it was grooved at the joints and braced at the ends, leaving but the very slightest crevice to admit the air. Nothing saved him from suffocation but the free use of the water—a quantity of which he took in with him in a beef's bladder, and with which he bathed his face—and the constant fanning of himself with his hat. He fanned himself unremittingly all the time. The "this side up" on the box was not regarded, and he was twice put with his head downward, resting with his back against the end of the box, his feet braced against the other,—the first time he succeeded in shifting his position; but the second time was on board of the steam boat, where people were sitting and standing about the box, and where any motions inside would have been overheard and have led to discovery; he was therefore obliged to keep his position *for twenty miles.* This nearly killed him. He says the veins in his temples were as thick as his finger. I had been expecting him for several days, and was in mortal fear all the time lest his arrival should only be a signal for calling in the coroner. You can better imagine than I can describe my sensations, when, in answer to my rap on the box and question, *"all right,"* the prompt response came "all right, sir." The man weighs 200 pounds, and is about five feet eight inches in height; and is, as you will see, a noble looking fellow. He will tell you the whole story. Please send him on to Mr. McGleveland, Boston, with this letter, to save me the time it would take to write another. He was boxed up in Richmond, at five, A.M. on Friday shipped at eight, and I opened him up at six (about daylight) next morning. He has a sister in New Bedford.

Yours, truly,

M. MCROY.

The report of Mr. Brown's escape spread far and wide, so that he was introduced to the Anti-Slavery Society in Philadelphia, from the office of which society a letter, of which the following is a copy, was written.

Anti-Slavery Office,
Philadelphia, April 8th, 1850.

H. Box BROWN,

My Dear Sir,—I was pleased to learn, by your letter, that it was your purpose to publish a narrative of the circumstances of your escape from slavery; such a publication, I should think, would not only be highly interesting, but well adapted to help on the cause of anti-slavery. Facts of this kind illustrate, without comment, the cruelty of the slave system, the fitness of its victims for freedom, and, at the same time, the guilt of the nation that tolerates its existence.

As one privy to many of the circumstances of your escape, *I* consider it one of the most remarkable exploits on record. That a man should come all the way from Richmond to Philadelphia, by the overland route, packed up in a box three feet long, by two and an half feet wide and deep, with scarcely a perceptible crevice for the admission of fresh air, and subject, at that time, to the rough handling and frequent shiftings of other freight, and that he should reach his destination alive, is a tale scarcely to be believed on the most irresistible testimony. I confess, if I had not myself been present at the opening of the box on its arrival, and had not witnessed with my own eyes, your resurrection from your living tomb, I should have been strongly disposed to question the truth of the story. As it was, however, seeing was believing, and believing was with me, at least, to be impressed with the diabolical character

of American Slavery, and the obligation that rests upon every
one to labour for its overthrow.

Trusting that this may be the impression produced by your
narrative, wherever it is read, and that it may be read wherever the evils of slavery are felt, I remain,

Your friend, truly,

J. MCKIM.

Were Mr. Brown in quest of an apology for publishing the following Narrative, the the letter of Mr. McKim would form that apology. The Narrative was published in America, and an edition of
8,000 copies sold in about two months, such was the interest
excited by the astounding revelations made by Mr. Brown as to the
real character of slavery, and the hypocrisy of those professors of
religion who have any connection with its infernal proceedings.

Several ministers of religion took a great interest in Mr. Brown, and
did what they could to bring the subject of his escape properly before
the public. The Rev. Mr. Spauldin, of Dover, N. H. was at the trouble
to write to two of his brethren in the ministry, a letter, of which the
following is a copy. The testimonials subjoining Mr. Spauldin's letter
were given by persons who had witnessed the exhibition.

TO THE REV. MESSRS. PIKE AND BROOKS.

Dover, 12th July, 1850

DEAR BRETHREN,

A coloured gentleman, Mr. H. B. Brown, purposes to visit
your village for the purpose of exhibiting his splendid
PANORAMA or *Mirror of Slavery*. I have had the pleasure of seeing it, and am prepared to say, from what I have myself seen,
and known in times past, of slavery and of the slave trade, in
my opinion, it is almost, if not quite, a perfect fac simile of
the workings of that horrible aud fiendish system. The real
life-like scenes presented in this PANORAMA, are admirably calculated to make an unfading impression upon the heart and

memory, such as no lectures, books, or colloquial correspondence can produce, especially on the minds of children and
young people, who should everywhere be brought before the
altar of Hannibal, to swear eternal hate to slavery, and love of
rational freedom. If you can spare the time to witness the
exhibition, I am quite certain you will feel yourselves amply
rewarded. I know very well, there are a great many impos-
tors and cheats going about through the country deceiving
and picking up the people's money, but *this* is of another class
altogether.

Yours, very truly,

JUSTIN SPAULDING.

I hereby certify that I have attended the exhibition of H. B.
Brown's Panorama, in this village, with very deep interest;
and most cordially subscribe my name, as an expression of
my full concurrence with the sentiment of the recommenda-
tion above.

A. LATHAM

I agree cordially in the above testimonials.

A. CAVERNO.

I am not an experienced judge in paintings of this kind, but
am only surprised that this is so well done and so much of it
true to the life.

OLIVER AYER PORRER,
Of Franklin-street, Baptist Minister.
Dover, N.H. July 15th, 1850.

Although the following letter, as to date, should have occupied a
place before the others, as it was addressed to the public and not to
any particular person, its present position will answer every purpose of its publication.

Syracuse, April 26th, 1850.

To THE PUBLIC,

There are few facts, connected with the terrible history of
American Slavery, that will be longer remembered, than that
a man escaped from the house of bondage, by coming from
Richmond, Virginia, to Philadelphia, in a box *three feet, one
inch long, two feet wide, and two feet six inches deep.* Twenty-seven
hours he was closely packed within those small dimensions,
and was tumbled along on drays, railroad cars, steam-boat,
and horse carts, as any other box of merchandize would have
been, sometimes on his feet, sometimes on his side, and once,
for an hour or two, actually on his head.

Such is the well attested fact, and this volume contains the
biography of the remarkable man, Henry Box Brown, who
thus attained his freedom. Is there a man in our country, who
better deserves his liberty? And is there to be found in these
northern states, an individual base to assist in returning him to
slavery! or to stand quietly by and consent to his recapture?

The narrative of such a man cannot fail to be interesting,
and I cordially commend it to all who love liberty and hate
oppression.

SAMUEL J. MAY.

After Mr. Brown's arrival in the Free States and the recovery of his
health, in addition to the publishing of his Narrative he began to
prepare the Panorama, which has been exhibited with such success
both in America and in England.

January, 1851.

We, the Teachers of St. John's Sunday School, Blackburn,
having seen the exhibition in our School-room, called the
"Panorama of American Slavery," feel it our duty to call upon

all our Christian brethren, who may have an opportunity, to go and witness this great mirror of slavery for themselves, feeling assured ourselves that it is calculated to leave a lasting impression upon the mind, and particularly that of the young.

We recommend it more especially on account of the exhibitor, Mr. Henry Box Brown, being himself a fugitive saave, and therefore able to give a true account of all the horrors of American Slavery, together with his own miraculous escape.

Signed,

John Francis,	John Alston,
John Parkinson,	George Fielding,
Henry Ainsworth,	Thomas Higham,
John Tomlinson,	Daniel Tomlinson,
Henry Wilkinson,	Benjamin Cliff,
John Hartley,	John Howcutt,
James Greaves,	James Holt,
John Roberts,	Mark Shaw,
Francis Broughton,	Christopher Higham.

Mr. Brown continued to travel in the United States until the Fugitive Slave Bill—which passed into law last year—rendered it necessary for him to seek an asylum on British ground. Such was the vigilance with which the search for victims was pursued, that Mr. Brown had to travel under an assumed name, and by the most secret means shift his panorama to prevent suspicion and capture.

THOMAS G. LEE,
Minister of New Windsor Chapel, Salford.
April 8, 1851.

NARRATIVE

OF THE

LIFE OF HENRY BOX BROWN

☞

Chapter I

I was born about forty-five miles from the city of Richmond, in Louisa County, in the year 1 8 1 5. I entered the world a slave— in the midst of a country whose most honoured writings declare that all men have a right to liberty—but had imprinted upon my body no mark which could be made to signify that my destiny was to be that of a bondman. Neither was there any angel stood by, at the hour of my birth, to hand my body over, by the authority of heaven, to be the property of a fellow-man; no, but I was a slave because my countrymen had made it lawful, in utter contempt of the declared will of heaven, for the strong to lay hold of the weak and to buy and to sell them as marketable goods. Thus was I born a slave; tyrants—remorseless, destitute of religion and every principle of humanity—stood by the couch of my mother and as I entered into the world, before I had done anything to forfeit my right to liberty, and while my soul was yet undefiled by the commission of actual sin, stretched forth their bloody arms and branded me with the mark of bondage, and by such means I became their own property. Yes, they robbed me of myself before I could know the nature of their wicked arts, and ever afterwards—until I forcibly wrenched myself from their hands—did they retain their stolen property.

My father and mother of course, were then slaves, but both of them are now enjoying such a measure of liberty, as the law affords to those who have made recompense to the tyrant for the right of property he holds in his fellow-man. It was not my fortune to be long under my mother's care; but I still possess a vivid recollection of her affectionate oversight. Such lessons as the following she would frequently give me. She would take me upon her knee and, pointing to the forest trees which were then stripped of their foliage by the winds of autumn, would say to me, my son, as yonder leaves are stripped from off the trees of the forest, so are the children of the slaves swept away from them by the hands of cruel tyrants; and her voice would tremble and she would seem almost choked with her deep emotion, while the tears would find their way down her saddened cheeks. On those occasions she fondly pressed me to her heaving bosom, as if to save me from so dreaded a calamity, or to feast on the enjoyments of maternal feeling while she yet retained possession of her child. I was then young, but I well recollect the sadness of her countenance, and the mournful sacredness of her words as they impressed themselves upon my youthful mind—never to be forgotten.

Mothers of the North! as you gaze upon the fair forms of your idolised little ones, just pause for a moment; how would you feel if you knew that at any time the will of a tyrant—who neither could nor would sympathise with your domestic feelings— might separate them for ever from your embrace, not to be laid in the silent grave "where the wicked cease from troubling and where the weary are at rest," but to live under the dominion of tyrants and avaricious men, whose cold hearts cannot sympathise with your feelings, but who will mock at any manifestation of tenderness, and scourge them to satisfy the cruelty of their own disposition; yet such is the condition of hundreds of thousands of mothers in the southern states of America.

My mother used to instruct me in the principles of morality according to her own notion of what was good and pure; but I had no means of acquiring proper conception of religion in a state of slavery, where all those who professed to be followers of Jesus Christ evinced more of the disposition of demons than of men; and it is really a matter of wonder to me now, considering the character of my position that I did not imbibe a strong and lasting hatred of every thing pertaining to the religion of Christ. My lessons in morality were of the most simple kind. I was told not to steal, not to tell lies, and to behave myself in a becoming manner towards everybody. My mother, although a slave, took great delight in watching the result of her moral training in the character of my brother and myself, whilst—whether successful or unsuccessful in the formation of superior habits in us it is not for me to say—there were sown for her a blissful remembrance in the minds of her children, which will be cherished, both by the bond and the free, as long as life shall last.

As a specimen of the religious knowledge of the slave, I may here state what were my impressions in regard to my master; assuring the reader that I am not joking but stating what were the opinions of all the slaves' children on my master's plantation, so that some judgment may be formed of the care which was taken of our religious instruction. I really believed my old master was Almighty God, and that the young master was Jesus Christ! The reason of this error seems to have been that we were taught to believe thunder to be the voice of God, and when it was about to thunder my old master would approach us, if we were in the yard, and say, all you children run into the house now, for it is going to thunder; and after the thunder storm was over he would approach us smilingly and say "what a fine shower we have had," and bidding us look at the flowers would observe how prettily they appeared; we children seeing this so frequently, could not avoid the idea that it was he that thundered and made the rain to fall, in order to make his flowers look beautiful, and I was nearly my eight years of age before I got rid of this childish superstition. Our master was uncommonly kind (for even a slaveholder may be kind) and as he moved about in his dignity he seemed like a god to us, but not withstanding his kindness although he knew very well what superstitious notions we formed of him, he never made the least attempt to correct our erroneous impression, but rather seemed pleased with the reverential feelings which we entertained towards him. All the young slaves called his son saviour and the manner in which I was undeceived was as follows.—One Sabbath after preaching time my mother told my father of a woman who wished to join the church. She had told the preacher that she had been baptised by one of the slaves at night—a practice which is quite common. After they went from their work to the minister he asked her if she believed that our Saviour came into the world and had died for the sins of men? And she said "yes." I was listening anxiously to the conversation, and when my mother had finished, I asked her if my young master was not the saviour whom the woman said was dead? She said he was not, but it was our Saviour in heaven. I then asked her if there was a saviour there too; when she told me that young master was not our Saviour;—which astonished me very much. I then asked her if old master was not he? to which she replied he was not, and began to instruct me more fully in reference to the God of heaven. After this I believed there was a God who ruled the world, but I did not previously entertain the least idea of any such Being; and however danger-ous my former notions were, they were not at all out of keeping with the blasphemous teachings of the hellish system of slavery.

One of my sisters became anxious to have her soul converted, and for this purpose had the hair cut from her head, because it is a notion which prevails amongst the slaves, that unless the hair be cut the soul cannot be converted. My mother reproved her for this and told her that she must pray to God who dwelled in heaven, and who only could convert her soul; and said if she wished to renounce the sins of the world she should recollect that it was not by outside show, such as the cutting of the hair, that God measured the worthi- or unworthiness of his servants. "Only ask of God," she said, "with an humble heart, forsaking your sins in obedience to his divine commandment, and whatever mercy is most fitting for your condition he will graciously bestow."

While quite a lad my principal employment was waiting upon my master and mistress, and at intervals taking lessons in the various kinds of work which was carried on on the plantation: and I have often, there—where the hot sun sent forth its scorch-ing rays upon my tender head—looked forward with dismay to the time when I, like my fellow slaves, should be driven by the taskmaster's cruel lash, to separate myself from my parents and all my present associates, to toil without reward and to suffer cruelties, as yet unknown. The slave has always the harrowing idea before him—however kindly he may be treated for the time being—that the auctioneer may soon set him up for public sale and knock him down as the property of the person who, whether man or demon, would pay his master the greatest number of dollars for his body.

Chapter II

My brother and myself were in the habit of carrying grain to the mill a few times in the year, which was the means of furnishing us with some information respecting other slaves, otherwise we would have known nothing whatever of what was going on anywhere in the world, expecting on our master's plantation. The mill was situated at a distance of about twenty miles from our residence, and belonged to one Colonel Ambler, in Yansinville county. On these occasions we used to acquire some little knowledge of what was going on around us, and we neglected no opportunity of making ourselves acquainted with the condition of other slaves.

On one occasion, while waiting for grain, we entered a house in the neighborhood, and while resting ourselves there, we saw a number of forlorn looking beings pass the door, and as they passed we noticed they gazed earnestly upon us; afterwards about fifty did the very same, and we heard some of them remarking that we had shoes, vests, and hats. We felt a desire to talk with them, and, accordingly after receiving some bread and meat from the mistress of the house we followed those abject beings to their quarters, and such a sight we had never witnessed before, as we had always lived on our master's plantation, and this was the first of our journeys to the mill. These Slaves were dressed in shirts made of coarse bagging such as coffee sacks are made from, and some kind of light substance for pantaloons, and this was all their clothing! They had no shoes, hats, vests, or coats, and when my brother spoke of their poor clothing they said they had never before seen colored persons dressed as we were; they looked very hungry, and we divided our bread and meat among them. They said they never had any meat given them by their master. My brother put various questions to them, such as if they had wives? did they go to church? &c., they said they had wives, but were obliged to marry persons who worked on the same plantation, as the master would not allow them to take wives from other plantations, consequently they were all related to each other, and the master obliged them to marry their relatives or to remain single. My brother asked one of them to show him his sister:—he said he could not distinguish them from the rest, as they were all his sisters. Although the slaves themselves entertain considerable respect for the law of marriage as a moral principle, and are exceedingly well pleased when they can obtain the services of a minister in the performance of the ceremony, yet the law recognizes no right in slaves to marry at all. The relation of husband and wife, parent and child, only exists by the toleration of their master, who may insult the slave's wife, or violate her person at any moment, and there is no law to punish him for what he has done. Now this not only may be as I have said, but it actually is the case to an alarming extent; and it is my candid opinion, that one of the strongest motives which operate upon the slave-holders in inducing them to maintain their iron grasp upon the unfortunate slaves, is because it gives them such unlimited control over the person of their female slaves. The greater part of slave-holders are licentious men, and the most respectable and kind masters keep some of these slaves as mistresses. It is for their pecuniary interest to do so, as their progeny is equal to so many dollars and cents in their pockets, instead of being a source of expense to them, as would be the case, if their slaves were free. It is a horrible idea, but it is no less true, that no slave husband has any certainty whatever of being able to retain his wife a single hour; neither has any wife any more certainty of her husband their fondest affection may be utterly disregarded, and their devoted attachment cruelly ignored at any moment a brutal slave-holder may think fit.

The slaves on Col. Ambler's plantation were never allowed to attend church, but were left to manage their religious affairs in their own way. An old slave whom they called John, decided on their religious profession and would baptize the approved parties during the silent watches of the night, while their master was asleep. We might have got information on many things from these slaves of Col. Ambler, but, while we were thus engaged, we perceived the overseer directing his steps towards us like a bear for its prey: we had however, time to ask one of them if they were ever whipped? to which he replied that not a day passed over their heads without some of them being brutally punished; "and" said he "we shall have to suffer for this talk with you. It was but this morning," he continued, "that many of us were severely whipped for having been baptized the night before!" After we left them we heard the screams of these poor creatures while they were suffering under the blows of the hard treatment received from the overseers, for the crime, as we supposed, of talking with us. We felt thankful that we were exempted from such treatment, but we had no certainty that we should not, ere long be placed in a similar position.

On returning to the mill we met a young man, a relation of the owner of this plantation, who for some time bad been eyeing us very attentively. He at length asked us if we had ever been whipped? and when I told him we had not, he replied, "well neither of you will ever be of any value." He expressed a good deal of surprise that we were allowed to wear hats and shoes, supposing that slaves had no business to wear such clothing as their master wore. We had carried our fishing lines with us and requested the privilege of fishing in his stream, which he roughly denied us, saying "we do not allow niggers to fish." Nothing daunted, however, by the rebuff, my brother went to another place, where, without asking permission of any one, he succeeded in obtaining a plentiful supply of fish and on returning, the young slave-holder seemed to be displeased at our success, but, knowing that we caught them in a stream which was not under his control, he said nothing. He knew that our master was a rich slave-holder and, probably, he guessed from our appearance that we were favorites of his, so perhaps he was somewhat induced, from that consideration, to let us alone, at any rate he did not molest us any more.

We afterwards carried our corn to a mill belonging to a Mr. Bullock, only about ten miles distant from our plantation. This man was very kind to us; if we were late at night he would take us into his house, give us beds to sleep upon, and take charge of our horses. He would even carry our grain himself into the mill; and he always furnished us in the morning with a good break-fast. We were rather astonished, for some time, that this man was so kind to us—and, in this respect, so different from the other miller—until we learned that he was not a slave-holder. This miller allowed us to catch as many fishes as we chose, and even furnished us with fishing implements when we had money for only very imperfect ones, of our own.

While at this mill we became acquainted with a coloured man from a northern part of the country; and as our desire was strong to learn how our brethren fared in other places, we questioned him respecting his treatment. He complained much of his hard fate; he said he had a wife and one child, and begged for some of our fish to carry to his wife, which we gladly gave him. He told us he had just sent a few hickory nuts to market for which he had received thirty-six cents, and that he had given the money to his wife, to furnish her with some little articles of comfort.

On our return from their place, one time, we met with a coloured man and woman, who were very cross to each other. We inquired as to the cause of their disagreement and the man told us that the woman had such a tongue, and that some of them and taken a sheep because they did not get enough to eat, and this woman, after eating of it, went and told their master, and they had all received a severe whipping. This man enjoined upon his slaves never to steal from him again, but to steal as much as they chose from any other person: and if they took care to do it in such a manner, as the owner could not catch them in the act, nor be able to swear to the property after they had fetched it, he would shield them from punishment provided they would give him a share of the meat. Not long after this the slaves availing themselves of their master's protection, stole a pig from a neighbouring plantation, and, according to their agreement, furnished their master with his share. The owner of the missing animal, however, having heard something to make him suspect what had become of his property, came rushing into the house of the man who had just eaten of the stolen food, and in a very excited manner demanded reparation from him for the beast which his slaves had stolen; and the villain, rising from the table where he had just been eating of the stolen property, said, my servants know no more about your stolen hog than I do, which indeed was perfectly true, and the loser of the swine went away without saying any more; but although the master of this slave with whom we were talking, had told him that it was no sin to steal from others, my brother took good care to let him know, before we separated, that it was as much a sin in the sight of God to steal from the one as the other, "Oh," said the master, "niggers has nothing to do with God," and indeed the whole feature of slavery is so utterly inconsistent with the principles of religion, reason, and humanity, that it is no wonder that the very mention of the word God grates upon the ear as if it typefied the degeneracy of this hellish system.

Turn! great Ruler of the skies!
Turn from their sins thy searching eyes;
Nor let the offences of their hand,
Within thy book recorded stand.

There's not a sparrow or a worm
O'erlooked in thy decrees,

Thou raisest monarchs to a throne—
They sink with equal ease.

May Christ's example, all divine,
To us a model prove!
Like his, O God! our hearts incline,
Our enemies to love!

Chapter III

My Master's son Charles, at one time, became impressed with the evils of slavery, and put his notion into practical effect by emancipating about forty of his slaves, and paying their expenses to a free state. Our old master, about this time, being unable to attend to all his affairs himself, employed an overseer whose disposition was so cruel as to make many of the slaves run away. I fancy the neighbours began to clamour about our master's mild treatment to his slaves, for which reason he was induced to employ an overseer. The change in our treatment was so great, and so much for the worse, that we could not help lamenting that the master had adopted such a change. There is no telling what might have been the result of this new method amongst slaves, so unused to the lash as we were, if in the midst of the experiment our old master had not been called upon to go the way of all the earth. As he was about to expire he sent for

my mother and me to come to his bedside; we ran with beating
hearts and highly elated feelings, not doubting, in the least, but
that he was about to confer upon us the boon of freedom—for
we had both expected that we should be set free when master
died—but imagine our deep disappointment when the old man
called me to his side and said, Henry you will make a good
Plough-boy, or a good gardener; now you must be an honest boy
and never tell an untruth.

I have given you to my son William, and you must obey him;
thus the old gentleman deceived us by his former kind treatment
and raised expectation in our youthful minds which were
doomed to be overthrown. He went to stand before the great
Jehovah to give an account of the deeds done in the body, and
we, disappointed in our expectations, were left to mourn, not so
much our master's death, as our galling bondage. If there is any
thing which tends to buoy up the spirit of the slave, under the
pressure of his severe toils, more than another, it is the hope of
future freedom: by this his heart is cheered and his soul is lighted
up in the midst of the fearful scenes of agony and suffering which
he has to endure. Occasionally, as some event approaches from
which lie can calculate on a relaxation of his sufferings, his hope
burns with a bright blaze; but most generally the mind of the
slave is filled with gloomy apprehension of a still harder fate. I
have known many slaves to labour unusually hard with the view
of obtaining the price of their own redemption, and, after they
paid for themselves over and over again, were—by the unprin-
cipled tyranny and fiendish mockery of moral principle in which
their barbarous masters delight to indulge—still refused what
they had so fully paid for, and what they so ardently desired.
Indeed a great many masters hold out to their slaves the object

of purchasing their own freedom—in order to induce them to labor more—without at the same time, entertaining the slightest idea of ever fulfilling their promise.

On the death of my old master, his property was inherited by four sons, whose names were, Stronn, Charles, John, and William Barret; so the human as well as every other kind of property, came to be divided equally amongst these four sons, which division—as it separated me from my father and mother, my sister and brother, with whom I had hitherto been allowed to live—was the most severe trial to my feelings which I had ever endured. I was then only fifteen years of age, but it is as present in my mind as if but yesterday's sun had shone upon the dreadful exhibition. My mother was separated from her youngest child, and it was not till after she had begged most pitiously for its restoration, that she was allowed to give it one farewell embrace, before she had to let it go for ever. This kind of torture is a thousand fold more cruel and barbarous than the use of the lash which lacerates the back; the gashes which the whip, or the cow skin makes may heal, and the place which was marked, in a little while may cease to exhibit the signs of what it had endured, but the pangs which lacerate the soul in consequence of the forcible disruption of parent and the dearest family ties, only grow deeper and more piercing, as memory fetches from a greater distance the horrid acts by which they have been produced. And there is no doubt but they under the weighty infirmities of declining life, and the increasing force and vividness with which the mind retains the memoranda of the agonies of former years—which form so great a part of memory's possessions in the minds of most slaves—hurry thousands annually from off the stage of life.

Mother, my sister Jane, and myself, fell into the hands of
William Barret. My sister Mary and her children went another
way; Edward, another, and John and Lewis and my sister Robinnet
another. William Barret took my sister Martha for his "keep Miss."
It is a difficult thing to divide all the slaves on a plantation; for no
person wishes for all children, or all old people; while both old,
young, and middle aged have to be divided:—but the tyrant slave-
holder regards not the social, or domestic feelings of the slave,
and makes his division according to the *moneyed* value they possess, without giving the slightest consideration to the domestic or
social ties by which the individuals are bound to each other; indeed
their common expression is, that "niggers have no feelings."

My father and mother were left on the plantation; but I was
taken to the city of Richmond, to work in a tobacco manufac-
tory, owned by my old master's son William, who had received
a special charge from his father to take good care of me, and
which charge my new master endeavoured to perform. He told
me if I would behave well he would take good care of me and
give me money to spend; he talked so kindly to me that I determined I would exert myself to the utmost to please him, and do
just as he wished me in every respect. He furnished me with a
new suit of clothes, and gave me money to buy things to send to
my mother. One day I overheard him telling the overseer that *his
father had raised me*—that I was a smart boy and that he must
never whip me. I tried exceedingly hard to perform what I
thought was my duty, and escaped the lash almost entirely,
although I often thought the overseer would have liked to have
given me a whipping, but my master's orders, which he dared
not altogether to set aside, were my defence; so under these circumstances my lot was comparatively easy.

Our overseer at that time was a coloured man, whose name was Wilson Gregory; he was generally considered a shrewd and sensible man, especially to be a man of colour; and after the orders which my master gave him concerning me, he used to treat me very kindly indeed, and gave me board and lodgings in his own house. Gregory acted as book keeper also to my master, and was much in favour with the merchants of the city and all who knew him; he instructed me how to judge of the qualities of tobacco, and with the view of making me a more proficient judge of that article, he advised me to learn to chew and to smoke which I therefore did.

About eighteen months after I came to the city of Richmond, an extraordinary occurrence took place which caused great excitement all over the town. I did not then know precisely what was the cause of this excitement, for I could get no satisfactory information from my master, only he said that some of the slaves had plotted to kill their owners. I have since learned that it was the famous Nat Turner's insurrection. Many slaves were whipped, hung, and cut down with the swords in the streets; and some that were found away from their quarters after dark, were shot; the whole city was in the utmost excitement, and the whites seemed terrified beyond measure, so true it is that the "wicked flee when no man pursueth." Great numbers of slaves were loaded with irons; some were half hung as it was termed—that is they were suspended from some tree with a rope about their necks, so adjusted as not quite to srangle them—and then they were pelted by men and boys with rotten eggs. This half hanging is a refined species of punishment peculiar to slaves! This insurrection took place some distance from the city, and was the occasion of the enacting of that law by which more than five slaves were forbidden to meet together unless they were at work; and also of that, for the silencing all coloured preachers. One of that class in our city, refused to obey the impious mandate, and in consequence of his refusal, was severely whipped. His religion was, however, found to be too deeply rooted for him to be silenced by any mere power of man, and consequently, no efforts could avail to extort from his lips, a promise that he would cease to proclaim the glad tidings of the gospel to his enslaved and perishing fellow-men.

I had now been about two years in Richmond city and not having, during that time, seen, and very seldom heard from, my mother, my feelings were very much tried by the separation which I had thus to endure. I missed severely her welcome smile when I returned from my daily task; no one seemed at that time to sympathise with me, and I began to feel, indeed, that I really was alone in the world; and worse than all, I could console myself with no hope, not even the most distant, that I should ever see my beloved parents again.

About this time Wilson Gregory, who was our overseer, died, and his place was supplied by a man named Stephen Bennett, who had a wooden leg; and who used to creep up behind the slaves to hear what they had to talk about in his absence; but his wooden leg generally betrayed him by coming into contact with something which would make a noise, and that would call the attention of the slaves to what he was about. He was a very mean man in all his ways, and was very much disliked by the slaves. He used to whip them, often, in a shameful manner. On one occasion I saw him take a slave, whose name was Pinkney, and make him take him off his shirt; he then tied his hands and gave him one hundred lashes on his bare back; and all this, because he lacked three pounds of his task, which was valued at six cents. I saw him do many other things which were equally cruel, but it would be useless to multiply instances here, as no rational being doubts that slavery, even in its mildest forms is a hard and cruel fate. Yet with all his barbarities and cruelties this man was generally reckoned a very sensible man on religious subjects, and he used to be frequently talking about things of that sort, but sometimes he spoke with very great levity indeed. He used to say that if he died and went to hell, he had enough of sense to fool the devil and get out. He did take his departure at last, to that bower, whence borne, no traveller returns, and whether well or ill prepared for the change, I will not say.

Bennet was followed as overseer, by one Henry Bedman, and he was the best that we had. He neither used the whip nor cheated the hands of what little they had to receive, and I am confident that he had more work done by equal numbers of hands, than had been done under any overseer either before or since his appointment to office. He possessed a much greater influence by his kindness than any overseer did by his lash. He was altogether a very good man; was very fond of sacred music, and used to ask me and some of the other slaves, who were working in the same room to sing for him—something "smart" as he used to say, which we were generally as well pleased to do, as he was to ask us: it was not our fate however to enjoy his kindness long, he too very soon died, and his death was looked upon as a misfortune by all who had been slaves under him.

Chapter IV

After the death of our lamented overseer we were placed under the care of one of the meanest and cruelest men that I ever knew; but before alluding particularly to his conduct, it may be interesting to describe the circumstances and condition of the slaves he had to superintend. The building in which I worked was about three hundred feet in length, and three stories high; affording room for two hundred people to work, but only one hundred and fifty were kept. One hundred and twenty of the persons employed were slaves, and the remainder free coloured people. We were obliged to work fourteen hours a day in the summer, and sixteen in the winter. One week consisted in separating the stems from the leaves of Tobacco; the leaves were then moistened with a fluid made from Liquorice and Sugar, which renders it not perfectly abhorrent to the taste of those who work it. These operations were performed by the women and boys, and after being thus moistened the leaves were then taken by the men and with the hands pressed into lumps and then twisted; it was then sent to what is called the machine house, and pressed into boxes and casks, whence it went to the sweat house and after lying about thirty days there, are taken out and shipped for the market.

The name of our overseer was John F. Allen; he was a thorough-going villain in all his modes of doing business; he was a savage looking sort of a man; always apparently ready for any work of barbarity or cruelty to which the most depraved despot might call him. He understood how to turn a penny for his own advantage as well as any man. No person could match him in making a bargain; but whether he had acquired his low cunning from associating with that clan, or had it originally as one of the inherent properties of his diabolical disposition, I could not discover, but he excelled all I had ever seen in low mean trickery and artifice. He used to boast that by his shrewdness in managing the slaves, he made enough to support himself and family—and he had a very large family which I am sure consumed not less than one hundred dollars per annum—without touching one farthing of his own salary, which was fifteen hundred dollars per annum.

Mr. Allen used to rise very early in the morning, not that he might enjoy sweet communion with his own thoughts, or with his God; nor that he might further the *legitimate* interest of his master, but in order to look after matters which principally concerned himself; that was to rob his master and the poor slaves that were under his control, by every means in his power. His early rising was looked upon by our master as a token of great devotedness to his business; and as he was with-all very pious and a member of the Episcopalian Church, my master seemed to place great confidence in him. It was therefore no use for any of the workmen to complain to the master of anything the overseer did, for he would not listen to a word they said, but gave his sanction to his barbarous conduct in the fullest extent, no matter how tyrannical or unjust that conduct, or how cruel the punishments which he inflicted; so that that demon of an overseer was in reality our master.

As a specimen of Allen's cruelty I will mention the revolting case of a coloured man, who was frequently in the habit of

singing. This man was taken sick, and although he had not made
his appearance at the factory for two or three days, no notice
was taken of him; no medicine was provided nor was there any
physician employed to heal him. At the end of that time Allen
ordered three men to go to the house of the invalid and fetch
him to the factory; and of course, in a little while the sick man
appeared; so feeble was he however from disease, that he was
scarcely able to stand. Allen, notwithstanding, desired him to be
stripped and his hands tied behind him; he was then tied to a
large post and questioned about his singing; Allen told him that
his singing consumed too much time, and that it hurt him very
much, but that he was going to give him some medicine that
would cure him; the poor trembling man made no reply and
immediately the pious overseer Allen for no other crime than
sickness, inflicted two-hundred lashes upon his bare back; and
even this might probably have been but a small part of his punishment, had a not the poor man fainted away: and it was only
then the blood-thirsty fiend ceased to apply the lash! I witnessed
this transaction myself, but I durst not venture to say that the
tyrant was doing wrong, because I was a slave and any interfer-
ance on my part, would have led to a similar punishment upon
myself. This poor man was sick for four weeks afterwards, during which time the weekly allowance, of seventy cents, for the
hands to board themselves with, was withheld, and the poor
man's wife had to support him in the best way she could, which
in a land of slavery is no easy matter.

The advocates of slavery will sometimes tell us, that the slave
is in better circumstances than he would be in a state of freedom, because he has a master to provide for him when he is sick;
but even if this doctrine were true it would afford no argument

whatever in favor of slavery; for no amount of kindness can be made the lawful price of any man's liberty, to infringe which is contrary to the laws of humanity and the decrees of God. But what is the real fact? In many instances the severe toils and exposures the slave has to endure at the will of his master, brings on his disease, and even then he is liable to the *lash for medicine*, and to live, or die by starvation as he may, without any support from his owner; for there is no law by which the master may be punished for his cruelty—by which he may be compelled to support his suffering slave.

My master knew all the circumstances of the case which I have just related, but he never interfered, nor even reproved the cruel overseer for what he had done; his motto was, Mr. Allen is always right, and so, right or wrong, whatever he did was law, and from his will there was no appeal.

I have before stated, that Mr. Allen was a very pious man— he was also a church member, but was much addicted to the habit of profane swearing—a vice which is, in slave countries, not at all uncommon in church members. He used particularly to expend his swearing breath in denunciation of the whole race of negroes—using more bad terms than I could here employ, without polluting the pen with which I write. Amongst the best epithets, were; "hogs," "dogs," "pigs," &c., &c.

At one time he was busily engaged in reading the bible, when a slave came in who had been about ten minutes behind his time—precious time! Allen depended upon the punctuallity of his slaves, for the support of his family, in the manner previously noticed: his anxiety to provide for his household led him to indulge in a boisterous outbreak of anger; so that when the slave came in, he said, what are you so late for you black scamp? The

poor man endeavoured to apologize for his lateness, but it was
to no purpose. This professing Christian proceeded to try the
effects of the Bible on the slave's body, and actually dealt him a
heavy blow in the face with the sacred book! But that not answer-
ing his purpose, and the man standing silent, he caught up a stick,
and beat him with that. The slave afterwards complained to the
master of the overseer's conduct, but was told that Mr. Allen
would not do anything wrong.

Amongst Mr. Allen's other religious offices, he held that of
superintendant of the sunday school, where he used to give frequent exhortations to the slaves' children, in reference to their
duty to their master. He told them they must never disobey their
master, nor lie, nor steal, for if they did any of these, they would
be sure to go to hell. But notwithstanding the deceitfulness of
his character, and the fiendishness of his disposition, he was not,
himself, perfectly proof, against the influence of fear. One day it
came on a heavy thunderstorm; the clouds lowered heavily, and
darkness usurped the dominion of day—it was so dark that the
hands could not see to work, and I then began to converse with
Mr. Allen about the storm. I asked him if it was not dangerous
for the hands to work while the lightning flashed so terribly? He
replied, he thought so, but he was placed there to keep them at
their work, and he could not do otherwise. Just as we were
speaking, a flash of lightning appeared to pass so close to us, that
Mr. Allen jumped up from where he was sitting, and ran and
locked himself up in a small room, where he supposed the lightning would not harm him. Some of the slaves said, they heard
him praying that God would spare his life. That was a very severe
storm, and a little while afterwards, we heard that a woman had
been killed by the lightning. Although in the thunderstorm

alluded to, Mr. Allen seemed to be alarmed; at other times he did not appear to think seriously about such things, for I have heard him say, that he did not think God had anything to do with thunder and lightning. This same official had much apparent zeal in the cause of the sunday school; he used to pray with, and for the children, and was indefatigable in teaching them the catechism after him; he was very particular, however, in not allowing them to hold the book in their own hands. His zeal did not appear to have any higher object than that of making the children more willing slaves; for he used frequently to tell his visitors that coloured people were never converted—that they had no souls, and could not go to heaven, but it was his duty to talk to them as he did! His liberality to the white people, was co-extensive with his denunciation of the coloured race; he said a white man may do what he pleased, and he could not be lost; he might lie, and rob the slaves, and do anything else, provided he read the bible and joined the church!

Chapter V

It may now be proper to say a little about the state of the churches in slave countries. There was a baptist minister in the city of Richmond, whose name was John Cave. I have heard this man declare in public, that he had preached six years before he was converted and the reason of his conversion was as follows.

He was in the habit of taking his glass of mint julep directly after prayers, or after preaching, which he thought wonderfully refreshed his soul and body; he would repeat the dram three or four times during the day. But an old slave of his, who had observed his practice hinted to him something about alternately drinking and preaching to the people; and, after thinking seriously on what the slave told him, he began to repent, and was converted. And now, he says he is truly converted, because his conscience reproved him for having made human beings articles of traffic; but I believe his second conversion is just about as complete as his first, for although he owed the second change to one of his own slaves, and ever confessed that the first effect of his conversion, was, to open up to his conscience the evil of the traffic in human beings, instead of letting those at liberty which he had under his control—and which might have been at once expected, as a natural consequence of his conviction—he endeavoured to apologize for the want of conscience, by finding, what he called, a good master for them, and selling them all to him.

But the religion of the slave-holder is everywhere a system of mere delusion, got up expressly for the purpose of deceiving the poor slaves, for everywhere the leading doctrine in the slave-holders' religion is, that it is the duty of the slave to obey his master in all things.

When Mr Carr left the city he was succeeded by a Mr. Jeter, who remained for many years; but at the time when he commenced his ministerial duties, many of the slaves were running away to free states; on the learning of which Mr. Jeter's first object was to devise some plan by which the masters could more effectively prevent their negroes from escaping; and the result of his ingenuity was as follows. He got the deacons and many more

of the good Christians of his church, whether to believe or not I
do not know, but to hold out that the place of meeting which
they then occupyed was not large enough for them; and he
seemed not to relish being in the same church with the negroes,
but, however that was, he managed, with the assistance of his
church members, to get the negroes all around the district to
believe that out of love for them, and from pure regard to their
spiritual interests, it had been agreed that the old meeting house
was to be given to the negroes for their own use, on their paying
a small portion of the price at which it was estimated. The
church was valued at 13,000 dollars, but they would only be
required to pay 3,000 dollars in order to have it for themselves.
The negroes were pleased with the idea of having a place of
meeting for themselves, and so were induced to save every cent
they could to buy the chapel. They were thus provided with a
strong motive for remaining where they were, and also by means
of this pious fraud, which it afterwards proved itself to be, they
were deprived of such little sums of money as might occasionally drop into their hands, and with which they might have been
assisted in effecting their escape. These resolutions were punc-
tually carried into effect; a splendid new church was built for
the whites; and it was made a rule of that church, that if any
coloured person entered it, without special business, he was
liable to be taken to the watch-house and to receive thirty-nine
lashes! The negroes paid what was at first demanded of them for
the old building, but when they wished to get it placed entirely
in their hands, they were charged with a still further sum; and
after they had paid that, they had still more to pay, and never, so
long as I was there, got possession of the church, and probably

never will. A minister was, however, appointed to preach for them beside the one that preached for the white people.

A man named Knopp who came from the north preached once in the church of the negroes. He took for his text, *"O! Jerusalem, Jerusalem which killest the prophets and stonest them that are sent unto thee, how often would I have gathered thee as a hen gathereth her chidkens under her wings, and ye would not."* Mr. Jeter and the members of the whites' church were so offended at this man's sermon, that they went in a body to his lodgings and were about to mob him, if he had not been defended by a number of his own friends, but I believe if he had been left to the tender mercies of this professed servant of the Most High, and his Christian associates, he would never have escaped with his life.

The Rev. R. Ryland, who preached for the coloured people, was professor at the Baptist seminary near the city of Richmond, and the coloured people had to pay him a salary of 700 dollars per annum, although they neither chose him nor had the least control over him. He did not consider himself bound to preach regularly, but only when he was not otherwise engaged, so he preached about forty sermons a year and was a zealous supporter of the slave-holders' cause; and, so far as I could judge, he had no notion whatever of the pure religion of Jesus Christ. He used to preach from such texts as that in the epistle to the Ephesians, where St. Paul says, "servants be obedient to them that are your masters and mistresses according to the flesh, and submit to them with fear and trembling"; he was not ashamed to invoke the authority of heaven in support of the slave degrading laws under which masters could with impunity abuse their fellow-creatures.

Chapter VI

I now began to think of entering the matrimonial state; and
with that view I had formed an acquaintance with a young
woman named Nancy, who was a slave belonging to a Mr. Leigh
a clerk in the Bank, and, like many more slave-holders, professing to be a very pious man. We had made it up to get married,
but it was necessary in the first place, to obtain our masters' permission, as we could do nothing without their consent. I therefore went to Mr. Leigh, and made known to him my wishes,
when he told me he never meant to sell Nancy, and if my master
would agree never to sell me, I might marry her. He promised
faithfully that he would not sell her, and pretended to entertain
an extreme horror of separating families. He gave me a note to
my master, and after they had discussed the matter over, I was
allowed to marry the object of my choice. When she became my
wife she was living with a Mr. Reevs, a minister of the gospel,
who had not long come from the north, where he had the character of being an anti-slavery man; but he had not been long in
the south when all his anti-slavery notions vanished and he
became a staunch advocate of slave-holding doctrines, and even
wrote articles in favour of slavery which were published in the
Richmond Republican.

My wife was still the property of Mr. Leigh and, from the
apparent sincerity of his promises to us, we felt confident that he
would not separate us. We had not; however, been married
above twelve months, when his conscientious scruples vanished,

and he sold my wife to a Mr. Joseph H. Colquitt, a saddler, living
in the city of Richmond, and a member of Dr. Plummer's church
there. This Mr. Colquitt was an exceedingly cruel man, and he
had a wife who was, if possible, still more cruel. She was very contrary and hard to be pleased; she used to abuse my wife very
much, not because she did not do her duty, but because, it was
said, her manners were too refined for a slave. At this time my
wife had a child and this vexed Mrs. Colquitt very much; she could
not bear to see her nursing her baby and used to wish some great
calamity to happen to my wife. Eventually she was so much displeased with my wife that she induced Mr. Colquitt to sell her to
one Philip M. Tabb, Junr. for the sum of 450 dollars; but coming
to see the value of her more clearly after she tried to do without
her, she could not rest till she got Mr. Colquitt to repurchase her
from Mr. Tabb, which he did in about four months after he had
sold her, for 500 dollars, being fifty more than he had sold her for.

Shortly after this Mr. Colquitt was taken sick, and his minister, the Rev. Dr. Plummer, was sent for to visit him; the doctor
came and prayed for him and so did other members of the
church; but he did not get any better so that they all thought he
must soon die; the doctors had given up all hopes of him, and his
wife and children, and friends, stood round his bedside in tears,
expecting every minute he would breathe his last. All the servants were in readiness lest they should be called to go on some
message. I had just then got home from labouring for my master; my wife was waiting for me, but she said she expected, every
minute, that some person would be calling to tell her that master was gone, when, to my surprise, Joseph Colquitt sent to my
wife to tell me to come and speak with him. I immediately left
my room and went to his bed-side; and as soon as he saw me he

caught hold of my hand and said;—"Henry will you pray for me and ask the Lord to spare my life, and restore me to health?" I felt it my duty to do the best I could in asking the Lord to have mercy upon him, because, although he was a slave-holder, and a very cruel man, and had used my wife very badly, yet I had no right to judge between him and his God, so I knelt down by his bed-side and prayed for him. After I got up he caught hold of my arm again and said, "one more favour I have to ask of you—go and tell all my slaves that belong to the church to come and pray for me." I went, according to his request, and we prayed three nights with him, after our work was done, and although we needed rest ourselves, yet at the earnest desire of the apparently dying man we were induced to forego our rest, and to spend our time in comforting him. At the end of this time he began to get a little better, and in a few weeks he was able to sit at table, and to take his meals with the family. I happened to be at his house one day, at our breakfast hour, after he got quite well, and his wife appeared as if she wished to joke her husband about the coloured people praying for him when he was sick. Mr. Colquitt had been expelled from the baptist church, and since that time she had disliked religion. She pretended that she did not believe either in God or Devil, and went on at such a rate, plaguing Mr. Colquitt, about the negroes praying for him, that he grew angry at last and exclaimed with an oath that it was all lies about the negroes praying for him; he denied asking any person to pray for him, and he said if he did ask the negroes to pray for him he must have been out of his senses, and did not, at the time he spoke, remember anything about it; but his wife still persisting in what she said, he went to the back door and calling his slaves one at a time, asked them who it was that prayed for him, until he got

the names of all those who had been concerned in the affair, and
when he had done so, he whipped every one of them which said
he had prayed as Mrs. Colquitt had stated. He seemed wishful to
whip me also, but, as I did not belong to him, he was deprived
of the pleasure of paying me for my services in the manner, in
which others had been rewarded. Mr. Colquitt, however, determined that I should suffer too, and for that purpose he proceeded
to sell my wife to one Samuel Cottrell, who wished to purchase
her. Cottrell was a saddler and had a shop in Richmond. This
man came to me one day and told me that Mr. Colquitt was
going to sell my wife and stated that he wanted a woman to wait
upon his wife, and he thought my wife would precisely suit her;
but he said her master asked 650 dollars for her and her children, and he had only 600 that he could conveniently spare but
if I would let him have fifty, to make up the price, he would prevent her from being sold away from me. I was, however, a little
suspicious about being fooled out of my money, and I asked him
if I did advance the money what security I could have that he
would not sell my wife as the others had done; but he said to me
"do you think if you allow me to have that money, that I could
have the heart to sell your wife to any other person but yourself,
and particularly knowing that your wife is my sister and you my
brother in the Lord; while all of us are members of the church?
Oh! no, I never could have the heart to do such a deed as that."
After he had shown off his religion in this manner, and lavished it
upon me, I thought I would let him have the money, not that I
had implicit faith in his promise, but that I knew he could purchase her if he wished whether I were to assist him or not, and I
thought by thus bringing him under an obligation to me it might
at least be somewhat to the advantage of my wife and to me; so I

gave him the fifty dollars and he went off and bought my wife and children:—and that very same day he came to me and told me, that my wife and children were now his property, and that I must hire a house for them and he would allow them to live there if I would furnish them with everything they wanted, and pay him fifty dollars, a year; "if you don't do this," he said, "I will sell her as soon as I can get a buyer for her." I was struck with astonishment to think that this man, in one day, could exhibit himself in two such different characters. A few hours ago filled with expressions of love and kindness, and now a monster tyrant, making light of the most social ties and imposing such terms as he chose on those whom, but a little, before, he had begged to conform to his will. Now, being a slave, I had no power to hire a house, and what this might have resulted in I do not know, if I had not met with a friend in the time of need, in the person of James C. A. Smith, Jr. He was a free man and I went to him and told him my tale and asked him to go and hire a house for me, to put my wife and children into; which he immediately did. He hired one at seventy-two dollars per annum, and stood master of it for me; and, notwithstanding the fearful liabilities under which I lay, I now began to feel a little easier, and might, perhaps, have managed to live in a kind of a way if we had been let alone here. But Mr. S. Cottrell had not yet done with robbing us; he no sooner saw that we were thus comfortably situated, than he said my wife must do some of his washing. I still had to pay the house hire, and the hire of my wife; to find her and the children with everything they required, and she had to do his washing beside. Still we felt ourselves more comfortable than we had ever been before. In this way, we went on for some time: I paid him the hire of my wife regularly, whenever he called for it—whether it was due or not—but he seemed still bent on robbing me more thoroughly than he had the previous day; for one pleasant morning, in the month of August, 1848, when my wife and children, and myself, were sitting at table, about to eat our breakfast, Mr. Cottrel called, and said, he wanted some money to day, as he had a demand for a large amount. I said to him, you know I have no money to spare, because it takes nearly all that I make for myself, to pay my wife's hire, the rent of my house, my own ties to my master, and to keep ourselves in meat and clothes; and if at any time, I have made any thing more than that, I have paid it to you in advance, and what more can I do? Mr. Cottrell, however said, "I want money, and money I will have." I could make him no answer; he then went away. I then said to my wife "I wonder what Mr. Cottrell means by saying I want money and money I will have," my poor wife burst into tears and said perhaps he will sell one of our little children, and our hearts were so full that neither of us could eat any breakfast, and after mutually embracing each other, as it might be our last meeting, and fondly pressing our little darlings to our bosoms, I left the the house and went off to my daily labour followed by my little children who called after me to come back soon. I felt that life had joys worth living for if I could only be allowed to enjoy them, but my heart was filled with deep anguish from the awful calamity, which I was thus obliged to contemplate, as not only a possible but a highly probable occurrence. I now went away to my work and I could as I went see many other slaves hastening in the same direction. I began to consider their lot and mine, and although my heart was filled with sorrow I felt still disposed to look upon the bright side of the future. I could still see some alleviation to my case of sorrow; it was true that the greater portion of my earnings were stolen from me by the unscrupulous hand of my master; that I was entirely at his mercy; and might at any moment be snatched from those enjoyments as well as those I thought were open to me; that if he chose he might still further gratify his robbing propensities and demand a larger portion of my earnings; so that the pleasures of intellect would be completely closed to my mind, but I could enjoy myself with my family about me while I listened to the pleasing prattle of my children, and experience the kindness of a wife, which were privileges that every slave could not enjoy.

I had not been many hours at my work, when I was informed that my wife and children were taken from their home, sent to the auction mart and sold, and then lay in prison ready to start away the next day for North Carolina with the man who had purchased them. I cannot express, in language, what were my feelings on this occasion. My master treated me kindly but he still retained me in a state of slavery. His kindness however did not keep me from feeling the smart of this awful deprivation. I had left my wife and children at home in the morning as well situated as slaves could be; I was not anticipating their loss, not on account of the feigned piety of their owner, for I had long ago learned to look through such hollow pretences in those who held slaves, but because of the obligation to me for money I had advanced to him, *on the expressed condition that he should not sell her to any person but myself*; such, however was the case, and as soon as I could get away, I went and purchased some things to take to the jail to them I so much loved; and to have one farewell embrace before parting for ever. I had not proceeded far however when I met with a gentleman who perceiving my anguish of heart, as depicted in my countenance, inquired what was the matter with me. I had no sooner hinted at my circumstances, however, than he knew all about it, having heard it, before. He advised me not to go to the jail, "for" said he "the man that bought your wife and family has told your master some falsehoods and has ordered the jailor to seize you and put you in prison if you should make your appearance there; when you would most likely be sold separately from them, because the *Methodist Minister* that bought your wife, does not want any men," so being thus advised I thought it better not to go to the jail myself, but I procured a friend to go in my stead, and take some money and the things which I had purchased for my wife, and tell her how it was that I could not come myself. And it turned out in the end to be much better that I did not go, for as soon as the young man arrived at the jail he was seized and put in prison, the jailor mistaking him for me: but when he discovered his mistake he was very angry and vented his rage upon the innocent youth by kicking him out of the prison. He discovered his mistake by asking my wife if that were not her husband, she said he was not; but he was not satisfied with her answer for he asked the children also if he were not their father, and as they too said no he was convinced, and then proceeded to abuse the young man in the manner before mentioned.

After I had heard of these things, I went to my *Christian* master and informed him how I was served, but he shoved me away from him as if I was not human. I could not rest with this however, I went to him a second time and implored him to be kind enough to buy my wife and to save me from so much trouble of mind; still he was inexorable and only answered me by telling me to go to my work and not bother him any more. I went to him a *third* time, which would be about ten o'clock and told him how Cottrell had robbed me, as this scoundrel was not satisfied with selling my wife and children, but he had no sooner got them out of the town than he took everything which he could find in my house and carried it off to be sold; the things which he then took had cost me nearly three hundred dollars. I begged master to write Cottrell and make him give me up my things, but his answer was Mr. Cottrell is a gentleman I am afraid to meddle with his business. So having satisfied myself that the master would do nothing for me, I left him and went to two young gentlemen with whom I was acquainted to try if I could induce them to buy my wife; but when I had stated my case to them they gave me to understand that they did not deal in slaves so they could not do that, but they expressed their willingness to do anything else that I might desire of them; so finding myself unsuccessful here, I went sorrowfully back to my own deserted home and found that what I had heard was quite true; not only had my wife and children been taken away, but every article of furniture had also been removed to the auction mart to be sold. I then made inquiry as to where my things had been put; and having found this out went to the sherriff's office and informed him, that the things Mr. Cottrell had brought to be sold did not belong to him, but that they were mine, and I hoped he would return them to me. I was then told by the sheriff that Mr. Cottrell had left the things to be sold in order to pay himself a debt of seventeen dollars and twenty-one cents, which he said if I would pay he would let me take away the things. I then went to my good friend Doctor Smith who was always ready and willing to do what he could for me, and having got the money, I paid it to the sheriff and took away the things which I was obliged to do that night, as far

as I was able, and what were left I removed in the morning.
When I was taking home the last of my things I met Mr. Cottrell, and two of his Christian brethren, in the street. He stopped
me and said he had heard I had been to the sherriff's office and
got away my things. Yes I said I have been and got away *my things*
but I could not get away *my wife and children* whom you have put
beyond my power to redeem. He then began to give me a round
of abuse, while his two Christian friends stood by and heard him,
but they did not seem to be the least offended at the terrible barbarity which was there placed before them.

I now left Mr. Cottrell and his friends, and going home, endeavored to court a little rest by lying down in a position so as to
induce sleep. I had borne too heavy a load of grief on my mind to
admit of me even closing my eyes for an hour during the whole
night. Many schemes for effecting the redemption of my family
passed through my mind, but when the morning's sun arose I
found myself on my way towards my master's house, to make
another attempt to induce him to purchase my wife. But although
I besought him, with tears in my eyes, I did not succeed in making
the least impression on his obdurate heart, and he utterly refused
to advance the smallest portion of the 5000 dollars I had paid him
in order to relieve my sufferings, and yet he was a church member
of considerable standing in Richmond. He even told me that I
could get another wife and so I need not trouble myself about that
one; but I told him those that God had joined together let no man
put assunder, and that I did not want another wife, but my own
whom I had loved so long. The mentioning of the passage of scrip-
ture seemed to give him much offence for he instantly drove me
from his house saying he did not wish to hear that!

My agony was now complete, she with whom I had travelled
the journey of life *in chains*, for the space of twelve years, and
the dear little pledges God had given us I could see plainly must
now be separated from me forever, and I must continue, deso-
late and alone, to drag my chains through the world. O dear, I
thought, shall my wife and children no more greet my sight with
their cheerful looks and happy smiles! for far away in the North
Carolina swamps are they henceforth to toil beneath the scorch-
ing rays of a hot sun deprived of a husband's and a father's care!
Can I endure such agony—shall I stay behind while they are thus
driven with the tyrant's rod? I must stay, I am a slave, the law of
men gives me no power to ameliorate my condition; it shuts up
every avenue of hope; but, thanks be to God, there is a law of
heaven which senates' laws cannot control!

While I was thus musing I received a message, that if I wished
to see my wife and children, and bid them the last farewell, I
could do so, by taking my stand on the street where they were
all to pass on their way for North Carolina. I quickly availed
myself of this information, and placed myself by the side of a
street, and soon had the melancholy satisfaction of witnessing
the approach of a gang of slaves, amounting to three hundred
and fifty in number, marching under the direction of a Methodist
minister, by whom they were purchased, and amongst which
slaves were my wife and children. I stood in the midst of many
who, like myself, were mourning the loss of friends and rela-
tions and had come there to obtain one parting look at those
whose company they but a short time before had imagined they
should always enjoy, but who were, without any regard to their
own wills, now driven by the tyrant's voice and the smart of the
whip on their way to another scene of toil, and, to them, another

land of sorrow in a far off southern country. These beings were
marched with ropes about their necks, and staples on their arms,
and, although in that respect the scene was no very novel one to
me, yet the peculiarity of my own circumstances made it assume
the appearance of unusual horror. This train of beings was
accompanied by a number of waggons loaded with little children
of many different families, which as they appeared rent the air
with their shrieks and cries and vain endeavours to resist the separation which was thus forced upon them, and the cords with
which they were thus bound; but what should I now see in the
very foremost wagon but a little child looking towards me and
pitifully calling, father! father! This was my eldest child, and I
was obliged to look upon it for the last time that I should, perhaps, ever see it again in life; if it had been going to the grave
and this gloomy procession had been about to return its body to
the dust from whence it sprang, whence its soul had taken its
departure for the land of spirits, my grief would have been nothing in comparison to what I then felt; for then I could have refl-
ected that its sufferings were over and that it would never again
require nor look for a father's care; but now it goes with all those
tender feelings riven, by which it was endeared to a father's love;
it must still live subject to the deprivation of paternal care and
to the chains and wrongs of slavery, and yet be dead to the pleasure of a father from whose heart the impression of its early
innocence and love will never be effaced. Thus passed my child
from my presence—it was my own child—I loved it with all
the fondness of a father; but things were so ordered that I could
only say, farewell, and leave it to pass in its chains while I looked
for the approach of another gang in which my wife was also
loaded with chains. My eye soon caught her precious face, but,

gracious heavens! that glance of agony may God spare me from ever again enduring! My wife, under the influence of her feelings, jumped aside; I seized hold of her hand while my mind felt unutterable things, and my tongue was only able to say, we shall meet in heaven! I went with her for about four miles hand in hand, but both our hearts were so overpowered with feeling that we could say nothing, and when at last we were obliged to part, the look of mutual love which we exchanged was all the token which we could give each other that we should yet meet in heaven.

Chapter VII

I had for a long while been a member of the choir in the Affeviar church in Richmond, but after the severe family affliction to which I have just alluded in the last chapter and the knowledge that these cruelties were perpetrated by ministers and church members, I began strongly to suspect the Christianity of the slave-holding church members and hesitated much about maintaining my connection with them. The suspicion of these slave-dealing Christians was the means of keeping me absent from all their churches from the time that my wife and children were torn from me, until Christmas day in the year 1848; and I would not have gone then but being a leading member of the choir, I yielded to the entreaties of my associates to assist at a concert of sacred music which was to be got up for the benefit of the church. My friend Dr. Smith, who was the conductor of the underground railway, was also a member of the choir, and when I had consented to attend he assisted me in selecting twenty-four pieces to be sung on the occasion.

On the day appointed for our concert I went along with Dr. Smith, and the singing commenced at half-past three o'clock, p.m. When we had sung about ten pieces and were engaged in singing the following verse—

Again the day returns of holy rest,
Which, when he made the world, Jehovah blest;
When, like his own, he bade our labours cease,
And all be piety, and all be peace,

the members were rather astonished at Dr. Smith, who stood on my right hand, suddenly closing his book, and sinking down upon his seat his eyes being at the same time filled with tears. Several of them began to inquire what was the matter with him, but he did not tell them. I guessed what it was and afterwards found out that I had judged of the circumstances correctly. Dr. Smith's feelings were overcome with a sense of doing wrongly in singing for the purpose of obtaining money to assist those who were buying and selling their fellow-men. He thought at that moment he felt reproved by Almighty God for lending his aid to the cause of slave-holding religion; and it was under this impression he closed his book and formed the resolution which he still acts upon, of never singing again or taking part in the services of a pro-slavery church. He is now in New England publicly advocating the cause of emancipation.

After we had sung several other pieces we commenced the authem, which run thus—

Vital spark of heavenly flame,

Quit, O! quit the mortal frame,—

these words awakened in me feelings in which the sting of former sufferings was still sticking fast, and stimulated by the example of Dr. Smith, whose feelings I read so correctly, I too made up my mind that I would be no longer guilty of assisting those bloody dealers in the bodies and souls of men; and ever since that time I have steadfastly kept my resolution.

I now began to get weary of my bonds; and earnestly panted after liberty. I felt convinced that I should be acting in accordance with the will of God, if I could snap in sunder those bonds by which I was held body and soul as the property of a fellow man. I looked forward to the good time which every day I more and more firmly believed would yet come, when I should walk the face of the earth in full possession of all that freedom which the finger of God had so clearly written on the constitutions of man, and which was common to the human race; but of which, by the cruel hand of tyranny, I, and millions of my fellow-men, had been robbed.

I was well acquainted with a store-keeper in the city of Richmond, from whom I used to purchase my provisions; and having formed a favourable opinion of his integrity, one day in the course of a little conversation with him, I said to him if I were free I would be able to do business such as he was doing; he then told me that my occupation (a tobacconist) was a money-making one, and if I were free I had no need to change for another. I then told him my circumstances in regard to my master, having to pay him twenty-five dollars per month, and yet that he refused to assist me in saving my wife from being sold and taken away to the South, where I should never see her again; and even refused to allow me to go and see her until my hours of labour were over. I told him this took place about five months ago, and I had been meditating my escape from slavery since, and asked him, as no person was near us, if he could give me any information about how I should proceed. I told him I had a little money and if he would assist me I would pay him for so doing. The man asked me if I was not afraid to speak that way to him; I said no, for I imagined he believed that every man had a right to liberty. He said I was quite right, and asked me how much money I would give him if he would assist me to get away. I told him that I had 166 dollars and that I would give him the half; so we ultimately agreed that I should have his service in the attempt for eighty-six. Now I only wanted to fix upon a plan. He told me of several plans by which others had managed to effect their escape, but none of them exactly suited my taste. I then left him to think over what would be best to be done, and, in the mean time, went to consult my friend Dr. Smith, on the subject. I mentioned the plans which the store-keeper had suggested, and as he did not approve either of them very much, I still looked for some plan which would be more certain and more safe, but I was determined that come what may, I should have my freedom or die in the attempt.

One day, while I was at work, and my thoughts were eagerly feasting upon the idea of freedom, I felt my soul called out to heaven to breathe a prayer to Almighty God. I prayed fervently that he who seeth in secret and knew the inmost desires of my heart, would lend me his aid in bursting my fetters asunder, and in restoring me to the possession of those rights, of which men had robbed me; when the idea suddenly flashed across my mind of shutting myself *up in a box*, and getting myself conveyed as dry goods to a free state.

Being now satisfied that this was the plan for me, I went to my friend Dr. Smith and, having aquainted him with it, we agreed to have it put at once into execution not however without calculating the chances of danger with which it was attended; but buoyed up by the prospect of freedom and increased hatred to slavery I was willing to dare even death itself rather than endure any longer the clanking of those galling chains. It being still necessary to have the assistance of the store-keeper, to see that the box was kept in its right position on its passage, I then went to let him know my intention, but he said although he was willing to serve me in any way he could, he did not think I could live in a box for so long a time as would be necessary to convey me to Philadelphia, but as I had already made up my mind, he consented to acompany me and keep the box right all the way.

My next object was to procure a box, and with the assistance of a carpenter that was very soon accomplished, and taken to the place where the packing was to be performed. In the mean time the store-keeper had written to a friend in Philidelphia, but as no answer had arrived, we resolved to carry out our purpose as best we could. It was deemed necessary that I should get permission to be absent from my work for a few days, in order to keep down suspicion until I had once fairly started on the road to liberty; and as I had then a gathered finger I thought that would form a very good excuse for obtaining leave of absence; but when I showed it to one overseer, Mr. Allen, he told me it was not so bad as to prevent me from working, so with a view of making it bad enough, I got Dr. Smith to procure for me some oil of vitriol in order to drop a little of this on it, but in my hurry I dropped rather much and made it worse than there was any occasion for, in fact it was very soon eaten in to the bone, and on presenting it again to Mr. Allen I obtained the permission required, with the advice that I should go home and get a poultice of flax-meal to it, and keep it well poulticed until it got better. I took him instantly at his word and went off directly to the store-keeper who had by this time received an answer from his friend in Philadelphia, and had obtained permission to address the box to him, this friend in that city, arranging to call for it as soon as it should arrive. There being no time to be lost, the store-keeper, Dr. Smith, and myself, agreed to meet next morning at four o'clock, in order to get the box ready for the express train. The box which I had procured was three feet one inch wide, two feet six inches high, and two feet wide: and on the morning of the 29th day of March, 1849, I went into the box—having previously bored three gimlet holes opposite my face, for air, and provided myself with a bladder of water, both for the purpose of quenching my thirst and for wetting my face, should I feel getting faint. I took the gimlet also with me, in order that I might bore more holes if I found I had not sufficient air. Being thus equipped for the battle of liberty, my friends nailed down the lid and had me conveyed to the Express Office, which was about a mile distant from the place where I was packed. I had no sooner arrived at the office than I was turned heels up, while some person nailed something on the end of the box. I was then put upon a wagon and driven off to the depôt with my head down, and I had no sooner arrived at the depôt, than the man who drove the wagon tumbled me roughly into the baggage car, where, however, I happened to fall on my right side.

The next place we arrived at was Potomac Creek, where the baggage had to be removed from the cars, to be put on board the steamer; where I was again placed with my head down, and in this dreadful position had to remain nearly an hour and a half, which, from the sufferings I had thus to endure, seemed like an age to me, but I was forgetting the battle of liberty, and I was resolved to conquer or die. I felt my eyes swelling as if they would burst from their sockets; and the veins on my temples were dreadfully distended with pressure of blood upon my head. In this position I attempted to lift my hand to my face but I had no power to move it; I felt a cold sweat coming over me which seemed to be a warning that death was about to terminate my earthly miseries, but as I feared even that, less than slavery, I resolved to submit to the will of God, and, under the influence of that impression, I lifted up my soul in prayer to God, who alone, was able to deliver me. My cry was soon heard, for I could hear a man saying to another, that he had travelled a long way and had been standing there two hours, and he would like to get somewhat to sit down; so perceiving my box, standing on end, he threw it down and then two sat upon it. I was thus relieved from a state of agony which may be more easily imagined than described. I could now listen to the men talking, and heard one of them asking the other what he supposed *the box contained*; his companion replied he guessed it was "THE MAIL." I too thought it was a mail but not such a mail as he supposed it to be.

The next place at which we arrived was the city of Washington, where I was taken from the steam boat, and again placed upon a wagon and carried to the depôt right side up with care;

but when the driver arrived at the depôt I heard him call for some person to help to take the box off the wagon, and someone answered him to the effect that he might throw it off; but, says the driver, it is marked "this side up with care"; so if I throw it off I might break something the other answered him that it did not matter if he broke all that was in it, the railway company were able enough to pay for it. No sooner were these words spoken than I began to tumble from the wagon, and falling on the end where my head was, I could hear my neck give a crack, as if it had been snapped asunder and I was knocked completely insensible. The first thing I heard, after that, was some person saying, "there is no room for the box, it will have to remain and be sent through to-morrow with the luggage train"; but the Lord had not quite forsaken me, for in answer to my earnest prayer. He so ordered affairs that I should not be left behind; and I now heard a man say that the box had come with the express, and it must be sent on. I was then tumbled into the car with my head downwards again, but the car had not proceeded far before, more luggage having to be taken in, my box got shifted about and so happened to turn upon its right side; and in this position I remained till I got to Philadelphia, of our arrival in which place I was informed by hearing some person say, "We are in port and at Philadelphia." My heart then leaped for joy, and I wondered if any person knew that such a box was there.

Here it may be proper to observe that the man who had promised to accompany my box failed to do what he promised; but, to prevent it remaining long at the station after its arrival, he sent a telegraphic message to his friend, and I was only twenty-seven hours in the box, though travelling a distance of three hundred and fifty miles.

I was now placed in the depôt amongst the other luggage, where I lay till seven o'clock, P.M., at which time a wagon drove up, and I heard a person inquire for such a box as that in which I was. I was then placed on a wagon and conveyed to the house where my friend in Richmond had arranged. I should be received. A number of persons soon collected round the box after it was taken in to the house, but as I did not know what was going on I kept myself quiet. I heard a man say "let us rap upon the box and see if he is alive"; and immediately a rap ensued and a voice said, tremblingly, "Is all right within?" to which I replied—"all right." The joy of the friends was very great; when they heard that I was alive they soon managed to break open the box, and then came my resurrection from the grave of slavery. I rose a freeman, but I was too weak, by reason of long confinement in that box, to be able to stand, so I immediately swooned away. After my recovery from the swoon the first thing, which arrested my attention was the presence of a number of friends, every one seeming more anxious than another, to have an opportunity of rendering me their assistance, and of bidding me a hearty welcome to the possession of my natural rights, I had risen as it were from the dead; I felt much more than I could readily express; but as the kindness of Almighty God had been so conspicuously shown in my deliverance, I burst forth into the following hymn of thanksgiving,

> I waited patiently, I waited patiently for the Lord,
>   for the Lord;
> And he inclined unto me, and heard my calling:
> I waited patiently, I waited patiently for the Lord,
> And he inclined unto me, and heard my calling:
> And he hath put a new song in my mouth,

Even a thanksgiving, even a thanksgiving even a
  thanksgiving unto our God.
Blessed, Blessed, Blessed, Blessed is the man, Blessed
  is the man,
Blessed is the man that hath set his hope, his hope in
  the Lord;
O Lord my God, Great, Great, Great,

Great are the wondrous works which thou hast done.
Great are the wondrous works which thou hast done,
  which thou hast done:
If I should declare them and speak of them, they would
  be more, more, more, than I am able to express.
I have not kept back thy loving kindness and truth from
  the great congregation.
I have not kept back thy loving kindness and truth from
  the great congregation.
Withdraw not thou thy mercy from me,
Withdraw not thou thy mercy from me, O Lord;
Let thy loving kindness and thy truth always preserve me,
Let all those that seek thee be joyful and glad,
Let all those that seek thee be joyful and glad, be joyful,
  and glad, be joyful, be joyful, be joyful, be joyful, be joyful
  and glad——be glad in thee.
And let such as love thy salvation,
And let such as love thy salvation, say, always,
The Lord be praised,
The Lord be praised.
Let all those that seek thee be joyful and glad,
And let such as love thy salvation, say always,
The Lord be praised,

The Lord be praised,
The Lord be praised.

I was then taken by the hand and welcomed to the houses of the following friends—Mr. J. Miller, Mr. McKin, Mr. and Mrs. Motte, Mr. and Mrs. Davis, and many others, by all of whom I was treated in the kindest manner possible. But it was thought proper that I should not remain long in Philadelphia, so arrangements were made for me to proceed to Massachusetts, where, by the assistance of a few Anti-slavery friends, I was enabled shortly after to arrive. I went to New York, where I became acquainted with Mr. II. Long, and Mr. Eli Smith, who were very kind to me the whole time I remained there. My next journey was to New Bedford, where I remained some weeks under the care of Mr. II. Ricketson, my finger being still bad from the effects of the oil of vitriol with which I dressed it before I left Richmond. While I was here I heard of a great anti-slavery meeting which was to take place in Boston, and being anxious to identify myself with that public movement, I proceeded there and had the pleasure of meeting the hearty sympathy of thousands to whom I related the story of my escape. I have since attended large meetings in different towns in the states of Maine, New Hampshire, Vermont, Connecticut, Rhode Island, Pennsylvania, and New York, in all of which places I have found many friends and have endeavored, according to the best of my abilities, to advocate the cause of the emancipation of the slave; with what success I will not pretend to say—but with a daily increasing confidence in the humanity and justice of my cause, and in the assurance of the approbation of Almighty God.

I have composed the following song in commemoration of my fete in the box:—

Air:—"Uncle Ned."

I

Here you see a man by the name of Henry Brown,
Run away from the South to the North;
Which he would not have done but they stole all his rights,
But they'll never do the like again.

   Chorus—Brown laid down the shovel and the hoe,
     Down in the box he did go;
     No more Slave work for Henry Box Brown,
     In the box *by Express* he did go

II

Then the orders they were given, and the cars did start
   away,
Roll along—roll along—roll along,
Down to the landing, where the steamboat lay,
To bear the baggage off to the north.
              Chorus

III

When they packed the baggage on, they turned him on

his head,
There poor Brown liked to have died;
There were passengers on board who wished to sit down,
And they turned the box down on its side.
                    Chorus

IV

When they got to the cars they threw the box off,
And down upon his head he did fall,
Then he heard his neck crack, and he thought it was broke,
But they never threw him off any more.
                    Chorus

V

When they got to Philadelphia they said he was in port,
And Brown then began to feel glad,
He was taken on the waggon to his final destination,
And left, "this side up with care."
                    Chorus

VI

The friends gathered round and asked if all was right,
As down on the box they did rap,
Brown answered them, saying, "yes all is right!"

He was then set free from his pain.

Chorus

APPENDIX

*The allusion in my song to the shovel and the hoe, is founded on the fol-
lowing story, which forms the share-holder's version of the creation of the
human race.*

The slave-holders say that originally, there were four persons
created (instead of only two) and, perhaps, it is owing to the
Christian account of the origin of man, in which account two
persons only are mentioned, that it is one of the doctrines of
slave-holders that slaves have no souls: however these four persons were two whites and two blacks; and the blacks were made
to wait upon the whites. But in man's original state when he neither required to manufacture clothes to cover his nakedness, or
to shelter him from storm; when he did not require to till the
earth or to sow or to reap its fruits, for his support! but when
everything sprung up spontaneously; when the shady bowers
invited him to rest, and the loaded trees dropped their luscious
burdens into his hands; in this state of things the white pair were
plagued with the incessant attendance of the two colored persons, and they prayed that God would find them something else
to do; and immediately while they stood, a black cloud seemed

to gather over their heads and to descend to the earth before them! While they gazed on these clouds, they saw them open and two bags of different size drop from them. They immediately ran to lay hold of the bags, and unfortunately for the black man—he being the strongest and swiftest—he arrived first at them, and laid hold of the bags, and the white man, coming up afterwards, got the smaller one. They then proceeded to untie their bags, when lo in the large one, there was a shovel and a hoe; and in the small one, a pen, ink, and paper; to write the declaration of the intention of the Almighty; they each proceeded to employ the Instruments which God had sent them, and ever since the colored race have bad to labor with the shovel and the hoe, while the rich man works with the pen and ink!

I have no apology whatever to make for what I have said, in regard to the pretended Christianity under which I was trained, while a slave. I have felt it my duty to speak of it harshly; because I have felt its blasting influence, and seen it used as a cloak under which to conceal the most foul and wicked deeds. Indeed the only thing I think it necessary to say in this place is what seems to me, and what may really be matter of serious doubt to persons who have the privilege of living in a free country, under the influence of liberal institutions; that there actually does exist in that land where men, women, and children are bought and sold, a church, calling itself the church of Christ; yes, my friends, it is true that the buyer and seller of the bodies and souls of his fellows; he who to day, can separate the husband from the wife, the parent from the child, or cut asunder the strongest ties of friendship, in order to gain a few dollars, to avert a trifling loss, or to please a whim of fancy, can ascend a pulpit tomorrow and preach, what he calls the gospel of Christ! Yes, and in many

cases, the house, which he calls the house of God, has been
erected from the price of human beings; the very stones of which
it is composed, have actually been dragged to their places by man
with chains at their heels, and ropes about their neck! It is not
for me to judge between those men and the God whom they pretend to serve, if their own consciences do not condemn them. I
pray that God may give them light to see the error of their ways,
and if they know that they are doing wrongly, that he may give
them grace to renovate, their hearts!

A few specimens of the laws of a slave-holding people may not
be out of place here; not that by such means, we can hope to convey a true idea of the actual condition of the people of these
places, because those matters on which the happiness or misery
of a people principally depend, and in general such matters as are
entirely beyond the reach of law. Beside—the various circumstances, which, independent of the law, in civilised and free countries, constitute the principal sources of happiness or misery—in
the slave-holding states of America, there is a strong current of
public opinion which the law is altogether incompetent to control. In many cases there are ideas of criminality, which are not
by statute law attached to the commission of certain acts, but
which are frequently found to exist under the title of "Lynch law"
either augmenting the punishment which the law requires, or
awarding punishment to what the law does not recognize as
crime—as the following will be sufficient to show.

"The letter of the law would have been sufficient for the protection of the lives of the miserable gamblers, in Vicksburg, and
other places in Mississippi, from the rage of those whose money
they had won; but gentlemen of property and standing, laughed
the law to scorn, rushed to the gambler's houses, put ropes

round their necks, dragged them through the streets, hanged
them in the public square, and thus saved the money they had
not yet paid. Thousands witnessed this wholesale murder, yet of
the scores of legal officers present, not one raised a finger to prevent it. How many hundreds of them helped to commit the murder with their own hands, does not appear, but many of them
has been indicted for it, and no one has made the least effort to
bring them to trial. Now the laws of Mississippi were not in fault,
when those men were murdered, nor were they in fault, that the
murders were not punished; the law demanded it, but the people
of Mississippi, the legal officers, the grand juries, and legislature
of the state, with one consent determine that the law shall be a
dead letter, and thus, the whole state assumes the guilt of these
murders, and, in bravado, flourish their reeking hands in the face
of the world; for the people of Vicksburg have actually erected a
monument in honor of Dr. H. S. Bodley, who was the ring-leader
of the Lynchers in this case."—*American Slavery as it is*.

It may be also worthy of remark, that in all cases in which we
have strong manifestation of public opinion, in opposition to the
law, it is always exhibited in the direction of cruelty; indeed, that
such should be the case, no person intimately acquainted with
the nature of the human mind, need be in the least surprised.
Who can consider the influence which the relationship of master
and slave—so extensively subsisting between the members of
slave states—in stimulating the passion and in degrading the
moral feelings, without being prepared to credit all that is said
of slavery? The most perfect abstract of the laws which regulate
the duties of slaves and slave-owners, must doubtless fail to convey any proper idea of the actual state of the slave; and the few
laws which we here cite, are not given for that purpose, but as a

sample of trash, which is called justice by slave-holders and quasi legal authorities.

"All negroes, mulattoes, or mertizoes, who now are, or shall hereafter, be in this province, and all their offspring, are hereby declared to be, and shall remain for ever hereafter, absolute slaves, and shall follow the condition of the mother."—*Law of South Carolina*.

The criminal offence of assault and battery, cannot, at common law, be committed upon the person of a slave, for, notwithstanding for some purposes, a slave is regarded in law, as a person, yet generally he is a mere chattel personal, and *his right of personal protection belongs to his master*, who can maintain an action of trespass, for the battery of his slave. There can be, therefore, no offence against the state for a mere beating of a slave, unaccompanied by any circumstances of cruelty, or an attempt to kill and murder. The peace of the state, is not thereby broken, for a slave is not generally regarded as legally capable of being within the pale of the State,—HE IS NOT A CITIZEN, AND IS NOT IN THAT CHARACTER ENTITLED TO HER PROTECTION."

"Any person may lawfully kill a slave who has been outlawed for running away and lurking in swamps, &c,"—*Law of North Carolina*.

"A slave endevouring to entice another slave to run away, if provision be prepared for the purpose of aiding in such running away, shall be punished with *death*: and a slave who shall aid the slave so endeavoring to run away, shall also suffer *death*."—*Law of South Carolina*.

"If a slave, when absent from his plantation, refuse to be examined by any white person, no matter what the moral character of such white person, or for what purpose he wishes to make the examination, such white person may chastise him, and if, in resisting his chastisement, he should strike the white person, by whom he is being chastised, he may be KILLED."—*Law of South Carolina*.

"If any slave shall presume to strike any white person provided such striking be not done by the command and in defence of the property of the owner, such slave shall, upon trial and conviction, before the justice or justices, suffer such punishment, for the first offence, as they shall think fit, not extending to life or limb, and for the second offence, *death*."—*Law of Georgia*.

"If any person cut any chain or collar, which any master of slaves has put upon his slave, to prevent such slave from running away, such person will be liable to a penalty not exceeding one thousand dollars, and imprisonment not exceeding two years."—*Law of Louisiana*.

"If any person cut out the tongue, put out the eye, cruelly burn, or deprive any slave of a limb, he shall be liable to a penalty not exceeding five hundred dollars."

"If a slave be attacked by any person not having sufficient cause for so doing, and be maimed or disabled so that THE OWNER SUFFERS A LOSS FROM HIS INABILITY TO LABOUR, the person so doing, shall pay the master of such disabled slave, for the time such slave shall be off work, and for the medical attendance on the slave."—*Law of South Carolina*.

Miscellaneous

If more than seven slaves be found together in any road without a white person, they shall be liable to twenty lashes each.

BIO BROWN

Brown, Henry Box, b.
1816.
Narrative of the life
of Henry Box Brown

06/10/21

CPSIA information can be obtained
at www.ICGtesting.com
Printed in the USA
LVHW032335210521
688195LV00004B/342

9 780195 148541